JOCK
of 40 Royal Marine Commando

My life from start to finish

JOCK
of 40 Royal Marine Commando
My life from start to finish

The autobiography of
ex-commando Jock Farmer

Shanklin Chine 2007

Copyright © Shanklin Chine
First published 2007
ISBN 978-0-9525876-5-1

Published by Shanklin Chine
12 Pomona Road, Shanklin
Isle of Wight PO37 6PF

Produced by Crossprint Design & Print
Newport, Isle of Wight PO30 5GY

Contents

		Page
Foreword		7
Acknowledgements		8
1	My family and my home	11
2	The Glen Cinema disaster	22
3	The post-war years of depression	27
4	I discover girls and war clouds gather	37
5	I answer the call to arms	43
6	The tough new Commando world	49
7	The disastrous Dieppe raid	59
8	A quiet interlude and love finds a way	70
9	The Sicily mission	80
10	Collapse of opposition and over to Italy	87
11	The fight for Termoli	93
12	Long train trek across Italy	102
13	To the Garigliano – I am wounded – news of Pops Manners' death	109
14	A rest in Malta and then we invade Sarande in Albania – Malaria recurs – then back to Turi	115
15	Christmas is a time for children – even in war	122
16	Our palace in Corfu – the last battle at Commachio	124
17	Serving brandy to the enemy – on the loose in Rome	131
18	Molly meets my family and we decide to marry	133
19	Back in uniform as a Territorial	138
20	I take the plunge and decide to set up on my own – 40 Royal Marines Commando Association (1942-1946) comes into being	142

*This book is dedicated
to all members, past and present,
of 40 Royal Marines Commandos*

Foreword
by Major General R D Houghton, CB, OBE, MC, DL

THIS IS THE moving life story of a young man, Jock Farmer, who was amongst the group of volunteers who formed the first of the famous Royal Marines Commandos, becoming one of a remarkable band of brothers, living and dying together during three years of relentless war and hardship, and creating a spirit of comradeship which remained to the end of their lives.

But it is more than that. The first chapters afford an inspirational insight into the life of a working class family in one of the bleak industrial towns of the North, revealing, despite their poverty, high standards of education, behaviour, honesty and loyalty which compare favourably with our modern anxiety about behaviour in the Britain of today. '

Then, in the final chapter, Jock, with no real Government help, had to recreate himself as a civilian and, despite or perhaps because of his wartime experiences, devoted a large part of his life to helping the community, and maintaining the old friendships, and memories of those who had fallen.

In my view Jock Farmer had a wonderful writing ability. I recommend this book to anyone interested in the history of war or our social history.

Robert Houghton
March 2007

Acknowledgements

JOCK FARMER was handed the final draft of his book three days before he died and his last words were to remind me to check some spelling!

I know that he would wish me to thank all his many friends for their encouragement and help in the preparation of this book and to mention, in particular, the late Peter Fisher whose support was so important to him. His family – Gary and Julie, (son and daughter), Krista (grand daughter), brother Tommy – were of enormous help in giving us access to family photographs. Also, Jock's cousin, Ellen Farmer, Honorary President of the Old Paisley Society, proved an invaluable source.

To General Robert Houghton a very big thank-you for his excellent Foreword and for reading the manuscript in its early and late days, suggesting alterations to vital passages.

To Adrian Searle, author of Shanklin Chine's book *PLUTO – Pipe Line Under the Ocean*, grateful thanks for his initial input and advice. And to my husband Michael, who had just published his first book, whose comments on the various drafts were much appreciated.

Major Jeff Beadle's excellent history *The Light Blue Lanyard - 50 years with 40 Commando Royal Marines* proved an invaluable source and we are immensely grateful for his wise guidance and support. Also to John Ambler, Royal Marines Museum, for his kindness and efficiency in arranging for us to use some of the images. I must also say thank-you to the Illustrated London News for allowing us to reproduce the picture of Monty with 40 RM Commando.

Grateful appreciation is due to Mike Lambert and his team at Crossprint for the excellent design and production – as always in a very short time.

And thank you, too, to Jock's friend Cecile Chard. who typed the first three drafts from his handwriting. She was followed by Jill Edwards of Shanklin Chine, who typed and retyped with patience and care.

But, above all, we owe an immense debt to Jock's Editor, Alan Morgan. This book could not have been published without his skill and expertise. Since 1994 Alan has been the brilliant designer of all our Exhibitions – he also served in the Army throughout the War. It was therefore inevitable that he and Jock should forge a wonderful working relationship. We were indeed lucky to have him as Jock's mentor.

For my part, I always saw the potential of Jock's book and am very glad to have been given the opportunity to publish.

Anne Springman
Owner of Shanklin Chine

1 My family and my home

I CAME into the world on 26th October 1921, number six in the family with two more to come. I was christened James after my dad, which was the recognised thing in those days. My elder brothers and sisters, in age sequence, were Robert, May, Bessie, Tommy and Margaret. The two younger ones to come were Bunty and Billy.

We lived in what were known as 'tenements'. They were usually three storeys high, with two apartments in each storey. They had two large bedrooms and a 'hole' in the wall bed in the sitting room. It would be an understatement to say it was rather crowded but with no bathroom and an outside toilet, my dear Mum kept us clean, clothed and well shod, which must have been hard work. As far as cleanliness was concerned, this was achieved by use of a large red bar of soap called Carbolic! It was used on all of us, especially Friday and Saturday nights when the large tin tub came out, placed in front of the fire on winter nights. Boys were Friday night and the girls Saturday. The same bar of soap washed our clothes, cooking utensils and ended up scrubbing the floor. Germs never came near and if they had, the smell would have killed them!

Our home was in Paisley, on the west coast of Scotland, with a population of around 100,000 at the time. There was little unemployment during my very young days as, within the boundaries of the town, were the huge thread mills. The Anchor Mills were in the centre of the town and the Ferguslie Mills were about a couple of miles away. The Ferguslie Mills were owned by the philanthropic family, named John Coats. Within the big estate the family owned, there were large stables housing horses, ponies and donkeys. The head groom was my maternal grandfather,

Thomas Grieve, who lived in a rather grand house called Ferguslie Lodge, which looked like a miniature castle and had an inside toilet.

In the town were Robertson's Jam Factory, Brown & Poulson Corn Flours and Creamola Custard Powder. There was also Dobie's Four Square cigarettes and tobacco and the famous at the time 'Paisley Tartan'. It was a mystery why it was called a tartan as it did not comprise checks and colours peculiar to the different clans. The main background was a deep maroon colour with 'swirls' of yellow, green and darkish blue which were almost psychedelic in shapes. Some of the larger shapes were like teardrops. Most of the production was used for ties and cravats. Sadly the factory went out of business before World War II.

About four miles away was the river Clyde, where the massive shipbuilding conglomerate John Brown and the engineering firm Babcock & Wilcox, closely aligned with each other and the numerous steelworks – all firms dependent on the building of ships. There were numerous smaller yards extending all the way down to Greenock. The huge cranes seemed to stretch away into infinity.

The house of my grandfather, groom to the John Coats' family. As well as its fancy architecture, it boasted an indoor loo!

My father was born in 1885, but it was the information on his birth certificate that aroused our curiosity. It stated that my paternal grandparents were married in County Fermanagh in Ireland in 1866, and their Protestant antecedents were brought over from Scotland to the northern part of Ireland to counteract the growth of the Roman Catholic Church. My grandparents left Ireland and settled in Paisley, where my father was born. The education given to the young must have been excellent, as my father was articulate and his handwriting copperplate. They say his betting slips were works of art. He started work at the age of fourteen driving a horse and cart for the Rope Works, later working for Coats Thread Mills. Being mechanically minded he progressed to driving lorries. My mother worked in the mills, so it was obvious how they met, and were eventually married.

When the 1914 war started, my Dad joined the R.A.S.C. as a driver and was one of the 'Old Contemptibles'. As he was away from home, my mother's parcels were much appreciated. He spoke of an instance when Mum sent him a half bottle of whisky, wrapped in two pairs socks but unfortunately the bottle had cracked and the precious liquid had soaked into the socks! He retrieved most of the whisky and sucked the socks for a couple of days before wearing them.

After the war, he went back to the mills for a while and then decided to work for himself. So with a horse and cart, he started selling fruit and vegetables. I believe he had a partner for a while. My eldest brother, Bobby, also worked for him during the holidays but knowing my Dad and my brother, it usually ended up as a comedy act. They would start arguing over some small thing and, when it was time to go home, Dad would sack Bobby. As he no longer worked for him, he had no right to ride on the cart and so he was forced to walk behind all the way home! Mum's comment was, "I have to stay married to the daft clown but you don't have to work for him".

Many years after my Dad had given up the fruit and vegetables business, my Mum and my two elder sisters confessed to him how they had 'swindled' him for years, if you can call it that. When they heard him coming up the stairs at the end of the day, they whipped the oil cloth off the table, just an ordinary affair, the top consisting of 6" x 1" planks of wood. My Dad emptied his money bag on the table and the female crooks casually spread the money over the table and, as 6d and 3d pieces were very small in those days, it was inevitable that some of them conveniently disappeared down the cavities between the planks. After a solemn counting up of the money, Dad took his beer money, had dinner, and when he had disappeared to the pub, the oil cloth was put back on. There was never all that much to hook out, Mum said, "There were only a few shillings and it was done for a laugh".

My father admitted that it was the events after the war that shaped his way of thinking. The working class in my father's generation were always part of a bonded work force. Although his foray into being his own boss had kept his large family well fed and shod, he realised his talents would be better served rejoining the work force and, during our many conversations, he explained his reasons. The civilian soldiers returning from the war were adamant that they were not going back to the Master and Worker conditions which preceded the World War, demanding better conditions and some form of contract applicable to their type of work.

His employment with the Paisley Co-operative Society not only secured the well-being of our family during the terrible years of the Depression, it helped the people around us by his ingenious methods of food distribution which, however small at times, were greatly appreciated. A man of strong principles, never using expletives, his one little weakness was Saturday night, coming home having imbibed too much of the national beverage. Laden with sweets for his large brood, and a large box of Chocolate Gingers for Mum, we usually ended up with a little sing-song. His strictness always had a smile on its face.

The discipline was left to our dear Mum, and was extremely comical at times. One afternoon, Tommy and I were having a rather loud argument directly underneath the kitchen window where Mum was washing clothes. She warned both of us to be quiet but, taking no heed, we carried on with our squabbling. The window opened and a full bath of warm soapy water descended on us. The window closed with not a word spoken. In the world of politics, my father was a paradox amongst his peers, as his thinking veered towards conservatism which in later years was a source of annoyance to my brother Tommy, who was an ardent socialist. My dear father died at the age of 76 and, on the day of his funeral, the place of remembrance was full to capacity with people from all walks of life; a sure testimony to a wonderful man, loved by his family and all who knew him.

(During World War II, when I was home on leave, I always met Dad at Paisley Co-operative garage where he then worked as a heavy lorry driver, bringing milk from the creameries at Kilmarnock through the night. He usually finished up grooming the beautiful Clydesdale stallions which pulled the milk carts, as he seemed to have a magic touch with them. It was always about noon when he finished and we would go for a pint at the Bowlers Tavern in Wellmeadow Street. During our conversations about almost everything, he gradually opened up my world, from the age of five to the declaration of war. My Dad was a very warm hearted man and I felt so much at ease with him).

We were going through very troubled times, especially during the Miners' Strike in 1926. As he worked for a construction firm at the time of the Strike, he felt it was nothing to do with him and the majority of men working with him agreed. They kept on working. As he explained, not only had he a large family to clothe and feed, there were a few disruptive groups, especially the communists, who were out to bring down the government of the country, not caring about the untold misery to the working class who, at that time, did not earn a large wage. The benefit system, which we enjoy today, was non-existent. If the wage earner did not work, he and his family did not eat.

The labour market was further complicated by the steady incursion of Southern Irish men. Driven from Ireland, where their families suffered abject poverty, mainly from their own government and the Roman Catholic Church, which had a stranglehold mainly on people who lived in the countryside. They undercut the local Scots, even by just a few pence, enough for jobs to be lost. The vast majority of the Scots on the west coast were staunchly Protestant and the bad feelings between them sometimes erupted into mini riots, usually on Friday nights, the Irish goading the Scots with taunts that they could take their jobs from them.

One such night, two Irishmen approached my Dad and boasted that on Monday morning he would be out of a job. My eldest brother took up the story. Just old enough to be able to drink alcohol, he was present on that occasion. "Dad took them out onto the main street and fought them, the result being the Irishmen ended up in hospital! The police duly arrived and, on hearing the full story, just walked away. Dad went to work as usual but by the end of the week, Mum noticed that he winced as he tried to lie down at night. She sent for the doctor who proclaimed that he had a broken rib! He had been driving a heavy lorry all week and, as far as he was concerned, this was no reason to give his employer any excuse to sack him!"

As a very young child certain instances burn in your memory and never leave. I clearly remember my Mother helping me to dress myself and telling me that she would be taking me to school for the first time, as I had reached the grand old age of five! I remember staring up at a rather stern looking lady who was seated on a very tall chair. I often wondered how she managed to get up there, as none of the children in the class ever saw her descend. Telling her my name, I was informed that she was Miss Grey. Thanking my Mother for bringing me, I was told to go to the top of the class, the reason being this was the only seat vacant.

The school was called Abercorn School. It was split in two, with the smaller section divided by a small wall barely two feet in height. Within the smaller premises were boys and girls who were rather backward in learning and who had special teachers. They were sent over the wall three mornings a week to intermingle with the children with normal learning abilities, with the idea that this would boost their ability to learn. The parents of the less bright children claimed that they could see a great difference in their learning by mixing with the other children. They became much more self-confident. We were far too young to have acquired the nasty habit of bullying and making remarks designed to make the children feel inadequate. We looked forward to them coming over the wall as it was a welcome diversion from the daily drag of learning the two-times-two table.

Near the end of the 1920's we moved from Incle Street to a more upmarket tenement in Hannah Street, about a mile away. The rooms were much nicer and, as our two eldest had flown the nest, there was more space. The front room had a new three-piece suite and was kept strictly for visitors, Christmas and the New Year. A couple of years after we moved in, I was found with my head stuck up the chimney trying to smoke a cigarette. Dad made me finish it and I never touched one again for a very long time.

I soon found out that Hannah Street was predominantly Protestant and the street running parallel with us, Clavering Street, was Catholic. Although the division that existed between Protestant and Catholic ran very deep, it only existed between the adults. The kids got on very well with each other. I had a child's curiosity towards the supposed differences and found very few. As large families seemed to be normal in those days, the streets always resounded to the cries of children, who formed into small gangs and then challenged each other to tests of "daring", as we called it. The most popular one was called "run sheep run" which involved tossing a coin to see who would do the 'run', which involved drawing a map on the payment with chalk. The map had to indicate running through three tenements in their backyards, climbing over the washhouses, back onto the main street and then a run to Paisley Cross, the distance of about a mile. Immediately the 'run' gang left, the opposing gang had to read the map and follow exactly the same route. If the opposition saw the 'run' gang before they reached the Cross, both gangs raced to the starting point over the same route to claim victory.

I now attended Craigielea School which was nearer to where

lived. The headmaster, Mr. Aird, was a very soldier-like man, always impeccably dressed with a 'Homburg' hat and neatly trimmed moustache and who, luckily for me, had a passion for teaching swimming to all the children. He explained it was the finest way to build young bodies and healthy bodies made healthy minds! I took to it like a duck to water. So I started going to the swimming baths every second night. The one great dividend it gained me was when Mum suddenly declared, "As you now look too clean to be true, you can skip the tub on Friday night". I started playing water polo, one of the most strenuous sports you could imagine. With knocks received in certain places of the anatomy, I could understand now why the adult lads sang soprano for a little while! This early introduction to sport training stood me in great stead years later during my Commando training, and played a large part in my survival as a would be Royal Marines Commando. I may only have been seven years of age at the time I am talking about and, with several gangs of youngsters roaming the streets, especially during summer holidays, the uninformed may think that mayhem ruled most of the time. But in the tenements, noise was part of our lives – silence only reigned when everybody retired to their beds and, as our parents knew, the streets were perfectly safe and the strong sense of honesty instilled into us made us never to indulge in petty pilfering.

I only 'bunked' off school once during my school days and, as it was the last day before the summer school holidays, it didn't seem such a terrible event and it really was my Dad's fault. I was nearly at the school gates when I heard the usual huffing and puffing noise of a steam lorry coming grunting towards me and then stop. My Dad shoved his head out of the cabin, crooked his finger at me and said, "Going to Edinburgh, Jimmy, want to come? We will go past the zoo and have a look at the animals and be back for supper. You've got nothing much doing today anyway". As it was such a monstrous machine, the driver's cab was quite high, so he had to lean over, grab me by the seat of my pants and deposit me on the seat opposite, and off we went on our travels. In those days, there were no huge housing estates blotting the landscape –

all you could see was green countryside with a few cottages huddled together and farmhouses galore.

It was a lovely day, the sun was shining and noticing my Dad's elbow sticking out of the side window, I immediately copied him! About half-way there, we stopped at a farmhouse that my Dad knew to get some homemade bread and butter and a huge chunk of cheese. He brought it out on a plate, slices of buttered bread and slices of very crumbly cheese. It was a meal fit for a king! Two deeply tea-stained tin mugs were produced, tea and sugar were added and, by placing them under the steam cock, we had instant tea. Even without milk, it tasted wonderful. But the best thing that was happening was that I had Dad all to myself. We eventually arrived at our destination, unloaded the building materials and, on our way back, Dad stopped on top of Corstorphine Hill to enable me to look down at the cages in the zoo. Corstorphine Zoo in later years acquired more land and was one of the first zoos to free the animals into open spaces where they could roam.

As we got nearer home, we stopped, had a quick mug of tea and as we were near a wheat field, Dad suggested that I go into the field and pick some poppies which invariably grew in wheat fields. He casually remarked, "You can give the poppies to your Mum because you are in trouble bunking off school". He started to laugh, knowing that the worst that would happen, I would get a thorough telling off. But I had the last laugh as we came in, Mum launched herself like a missile onto Dad, thumping him on the arms, crying, "Don't you realise that tearing around Scotland is not the thing to do with a boy who should be in school and to be told by a teacher where he had disappeared to". I decided to creep away whilst this was going on, smiling at the idea of 'tearing' around the country when the old 'steamer's' top speed was 25 m.p.h. I didn't get off as lightly as I thought I had. After supper, I was ordered to bed. As the sun was still shining, I could hear the other kids having a game of rounders, so I consoled myself that I had had a great adventure with my Dad, buried myself in the blankets and relived the day.

At Christmas our presents, eagerly awaited, were never of

great value but it was the sense of excitement that made this time of the year so different. When I was about five, I was given a huge Meccano set, previously the property of my cousin, Jim Morrison. He was a careful youngster, and the set was complete. Mum lit the fire in the posh sitting room so that I could spread out the numerous parts of all shapes and sizes as Jim had added to the original box across the years.

I acquired an old grandfather clock face that had been slung out by the watchmaker in Well Street. The ratchet that had held the masses of wheels in check was missing. Consequently when it was wound up, it rapidly unwound itself. By building a supposed racing car and attaching it to the rear wheels, then winding the whole ensemble and letting go, it shot forward like a bullet. I was extremely proud of myself.

On the last day of 1928, every household in the tenements was busy, upholding the old Scottish tradition of beginning the New Year with a clean face. Curtains were replaced with fresh ones,

My parents, to whom I owe so much, at their Golden Wedding celebration.

floors were scrubbed, and new bed linen on the beds. The ovens were black leaded and by ten o'clock in the evening, everybody in the household was in their best Sunday clothes. Mum had baked the usual shortbreads and made about a gallon of ginger wine (non alcoholic) for the youngsters. The whisky and the beer were laid neatly on the table and there were plenty of sandwiches for the visitors and friends. The pubs closed their doors at ten, so we expected Dad about 10.30, well oiled, usually with a small trail of obscure relatives who seemed to have no home to go to. Bobby was the one to 'First Foot', as he was darker than the rest of us, armed with a piece of coal signifying there will always be a fire in the grate, a two shilling coin so that we would never be poor, and a piece of cake so that we would never be hungry. He always knocked at the door one minute past twelve - and God help him if he was ever late!

Although one year younger, Tommy had left school and found a job in a grocer's shop. He had to work late, and I suspect had girl trouble. He didn't judge the time properly and just reached our gate when the bells started to ring. He shouted up to the window to be let in but Mum told him he had to stay out until Bobby arrived! To make matters worse, it had started to rain quite heavily. He started to shout again to be let in as he was getting soaked. Mum raised the window and calmly told him that as it was raining, it was quite obvious he was going to get wet and shut the window. Bobby arrived about half an hour later, slightly the worse for wear and spied Tommy by the gate looking like a drowned rat. Mum kept a wary eye from the window and ordered both of them indoors, Bobby first! Mum got Tommy dry clothes and gave him a good rubbing down until he was as good as new and joined in the banter. As the adults toasted each other with whisky, the kids solemnly touched each other's glasses filled with ginger wine.

2 The Glen Cinema disaster

CHILDREN my age and above could never forget Hogmanay, the last day of 1929. It transpired to be the most sorrowful and heart-rending day in the history of Paisley. I awoke to the smell of bacon and knowing that there would be thick potato scones frying alongside and a bowl of porridge first, it was a good start to the day. With no school, things couldn't be better. I nudged Tommy and during our chatter both agreed we would be extra nice to Mum and then she might give us two pence each, the cost of admission to the Glen Cinema in the afternoon. The proprietors of the Glen Cinema had a strange but effective monetary system. One paid two pence in cash, or three jam jars, and the jam jars being worth one penny each, they were making an extra penny on each person. Their reasoning was that it took time to separate them and to take the jars back to the respective shops.

It was quite a common occurrence for lads to climb the walls at the rear of grocers' shops and lift three jam jars to gain admission to the cinema. We did not consider it thieving. We were just helping ourselves and by way of absolution, the jars ended up in the backyard where they came from in the first place. Once, one of the lads in our tenement was a jar short, so he emptied half a jar of marmalade down the toilet to enable him to accompany us to see the great cowboy, Tom Mix. When we got home, I could hear quite a few yelps coming from his kitchen. We noted the next day that he would rather stand than sit. The rest of the lads tried to imagine what his 'bum' looked like. We all came to the same conclusion – that it would be from a very pale pink to a very deep red!

Tommy and I enjoyed a wonderful breakfast and volunteered to wash the dishes and carry out any chore that Mum wanted doing. Telling us to stay out of trouble, she gave us two pence each and an extra farthing for sweets. She did not even mention the cinema. We both agreed to be careful of our thoughts when we were at home, otherwise we would be delivered a smack on the backside. We were positive she could read our minds!

That morning the lads from Clavering Street came round to challenge us to a game of rounders (same as baseball) . We retired to the waste ground straddling both our streets and, for two hours, it was sheer bedlam. In the countless games we played against each other, not once did neither team win, as always a fight started or the ball was conveniently lost. The fact was that neither side wanted to lose and if they saw that was going to happen, any small irregularity was pounced on and the game soon ended. Years later, these games were the source of many happy memories.

Willie Pettigrew came round later, with his tuppence and a farthing, so the three of us set out for the cinema in plenty of time. We decided to pool our farthings and visit Lipton's, the largest grocers in Paisley, who regularly had a large barrel of broken biscuits just inside the store. We barely started when Tommy had a change of heart and decided to go to the football match, St Mirren against Kilmarnock, which was always played on New Year's Day. Willie and I carried on to Lipton's, duly paid our combined wealth, collected two paper bags, were instructed "half full only" and no sticking grubby hands into the barrel trying to find the ginger, jam or cream ones. From the top only, or clear off. So between half filling our bags and stuffing our mouths at the same time, we decided not to rush to get into the Glen as the kids with money got preference over the jam jars. We were sauntering down Wellmeadow Street, not making any conversation for obvious reasons, when we spied a group of well-dressed people with buttonholes entering the local church, so we made speed towards it.

The wonderful Scots' custom during weddings was that when the bride and bridegroom were married, and before driving away, they threw handfuls of halfpennies out of the taxi, spreading them all over the pavement. As there were other kids there and being old hands at this game, we stayed on the outside of the others, in the direction of departing taxis, as the coins tended to fly in that direction. We shared the spoils and ended up with ten pence each. We made our way towards the Glen Cinema but, alas, we were too late! The gates were shut. As it wasn't very warm, although we wore ample clothes, we boarded a tram, paid a penny, and stayed on till the conductor told us to get off. We crossed the road and took the next tram back home. I opened the door, walked into the kitchen and Mum let out a scream, whacked me so hard that I went on my knees. Within seconds she was cuddling me, crying at the same time. It was too much for me, getting a slap and then a cuddle, whatever next? Bessie took me into the front room and told me that the Glen Cinema was on fire and many children were dead! Mum, knowing I was going there, was beside herself, thinking the worst, and just lost herself when she saw me. Tommy had called home after the match, so he escaped the wrath and the joy of a desperate Mum. Tea time was a muted affair and when I asked where Dad was, Mum just said, "He's helping". We were getting ready for bed when Dad came in. It was one of the many instances that however young a person is, it burns into his brain and remains forever. His face and hands were black and instead of his soldier's stance, he seemed to stoop. His whole demeanour was of sadness and defeat. He sat down on his chair and silently wept, his strong body shook. Mum quietly pointed to the bedroom and we did as we were told, fell asleep, and slept as soundly as any other night. Luckily, being a child, the grim horrors of that day, 31 January 1929, did not penetrate our young minds. From then on, the immediate future was just a blur. The kids were soon as noisy as ever and the adults seemed to encourage it as if to make up for the missing voices.

 I was about fifteen when I mentioned to Mum that one had to be sixteen before being allowed to learn ballroom dancing at the Dance Academy and, in turn, had to have a pass from said establishment to enable one to enter the grand portals of the Town Hall Ballroom.

On mentioning the Dance Academy, Mum told me to sit down and then told me, that watching all the mothers, whether they had lost children or not, grieving was widespread throughout the town. Protestants and Catholics wept on each other's shoulders. When all the children who had paid, cash or jars, a terrible mistake was made. All the doors were locked in a stupid effort to stop kids creeping in when the lights went out. Seventy-one children were lost. Mum spoke of the businesses, large and small, who carried on half heartedly during the weeks after the children were laid to rest. Among them was Martha Gibson, my cousin, aged ten, who died that terrible day. There had been no fire. The children had been asphyxiated by fumes from the projection room.

It was decided to pull the Cinema down to the ground. In its place, a bright modern building was built. Burton's, the tailors for men, occupied the ground floor and the top floor was the Dance Academy, the name that evoked Mum's memory of that terrible day.

In sad procession, a line of taxis carry the coffins of the children past the Glen Cinema where they had died.

Fourteen years later, when Dad and I were comfortably ensconced in the Bowlers sipping our pints, I casually remarked that Willie Pettigrew had joined the Navy. Without thinking, I said, "If it wasn't for the wedding, we would have gone to the 'Glen' that day." As soon as I said it, I felt the colour rush to my face and struggled to say something else but Dad, sensing my discomfiture, touched me and said, "It's about time I spoke about it – I was told about 3.30 in the afternoon what was happening. I volunteered to take my lorry there, as it was covered, and when I got to the cinema I had to take it up close to the entrance. Black smoke was pouring out from every opening and I had to enter the building to help the firemen bring out the wee souls. Even the firemen were crying. I was scared to look at the faces because I was mortally afraid that Tommy and yourself were in there somewhere. After a short while as I came out, I saw Bessie in the crowd who shouted, it's all right! I felt almost guilty as a surge of relief went through me."

He suddenly stopped and told me to drink up as we were late for dinner and didn't want to be used as a punch bag again, alluding to our Edinburgh escapade!

The memorial to the seventy-one children who died in the Hogmanay disaster.

3 The post-war years of depression

TOWARDS the end of 1929, there was an alarming decline in every branch of business, from the large industries to the small, who invariably depended on the former. It was the start of the world wide depression which brought misery and hunger in its wake. But whatever was happening in the world, it was Hannah Street and the few streets immediately around us that mattered. In Mum's words, "It was the mothers around us who waited with dread every evening for their man to come home and declare that they still had a job". Mum always said 'mothers' never 'women'.

By 1931, the depression had bitten deeply into the families around us. Out of the six families in our tenement, only Dad was still working and then one day it happened! Dad came in, threw his cap on the table, and said to my Mum, "I am out of a job, Bessie". But the luck of the Farmers still held. It wasn't long before my Dad got a call from my uncle, Jim Morrison, who had become head of transport for the Paisley Co-operative Society. They embraced a chain of grocery and bakery shops and had a huge milk delivery round and a funeral service. He was told that the reason he was now working for the Co-op was because he could drive any kind of vehicle, small, large, petrol, steam or articulated. His way with the magnificent Clydesdales (huge stallions) which pulled the milk carts was well known. Dad also drove the Rolls Royce hearses to funerals, suitably attired in dark suit, white shirt and black tie.

There was an amusing episode one day when Dad took the hearse to go to the bereaved house. As he was a bit early, he stopped at the Swan Inn in Smithfield Street for a pint. Getting into conversation with a friend, he forgot the time and ended up arriving twenty minutes late to collect the deceased, then a dash to church. The irate mourners complained that the service would have be shortened, as there was another service immediately afterwards. Dad spoke to a person he knew and said, "I'm quite sure Danny, who is in the box, couldn't give a tuppenny curse". Then the funeral procession literally 'took off'. Dad said later it was a good job the coffin was well secured, as the times he had to brake it nearly landed in beside him.

The biggest belly laugh we ever had with Dad's exploits was when he was doing milk rounds during the summer and he had struck up a wonderful relationship with a Clydesdale mare called Nellie. It only had to hear Dad's footsteps, and it would start neighing loudly and without restrainers would walk towards the milk cart and back itself in without assistance. The milk round always finished in Smithhill Street, so invariably Nellie was left standing outside the Swan Inn whilst Dad enjoyed his beer. But Nellie was never forgotten and she was given a bucket full of water with a generous helping of beer. This happened every day except Sunday.

Then came the time for Dad to have his two weeks' holiday. With a loan of the largest taxi in the garage, Mum, Dad and five kids made for Newton on Ayr, a seaside resort. We proceeded to enjoy every second, loving all the pleasures of the seaside. In the evenings, as our apartment overlooked a dog track, we sat by the window betting farthings on the greyhounds in the race. Back in Paisley there were hilarious goings on with Dad's milk round. The man who took over found it was quite easy until, in his own words, "I came into Smithhill Street, finished my last delivery, went trotting up the street, then came to a shuddering halt at the Swan Inn and Nellie refused to move, disregarding threats, curses and thumps on her rear. She was determined not to move! Hearing what was going on outside, the landlord came out and sizing up the situation, invited the man inside for a drink, "take a bucket of water with some beer for Nellie and then go on your way". The trouble with Bob Ferguson was that he was a staunch Methodist and did not indulge in alcohol. So for a few minutes there was a stand off – a man who resolutely would not enter a pub, and a huge horse who would not budge until she had had her morning treat. It wasn't until the landlord realised that his customers were all outside rather than in, watching the comical proceedings and not drinking his beer, that he forced Bob Ferguson to forget his high principles and agree to enter through the Public Bar and exit through the Lounge Bar, collecting on his way Nellie's bucket and, when finished, to deposit it inside the Lounge porch. The alternative would be to telephone his employers and explain the situation, which would make Bob look rather silly in the workplace. Immediately he had done this, he jumped aboard the milk cart and Nellie set off at a steady trot, breaking wind on the way. (Nellie's way of expressing her feelings?) The lads in the stables didn't like to tell Bob that, as he wrestled with Nellie in the morning trying to get her in between the shafts, all he had to do was stand with the reins and Nellie would go in by herself! Poor Bob Ferguson – he endured twelve days of purgatory before Dad came back and he was never the same again.

On another occasion, I was with Dad on a Saturday morning (before I started a milk round myself) when we came to a busy junction at Silk Street. Dad was busy writing out his betting slip for horse racing when he suddenly realised that Nellie had stopped. He shouted at the horse, "For God's sake move, you silly old bugger, you can see there's nothing coming." Life was never dull!

In the same street was the Paisley Theatre which promoted amateur plays. Friday nights were amateur nights when singers, acrobats, strong men and so on would take to the stage and hopefully be on their way to a career in show business. They all knew that they were in for a very rough time on the Paisley stage! The admittance on Friday nights was only three pence for adults and one penny for children. Our seating arrangement was in the 'gods' which was a simple row of long seats in alignment with the steps, which meant that the person behind you with his or her muddy boots would be tickling your ears.

As the brave souls took to the stage, the raucous shouting

from the 'gods' drowned them out. Some of the acts stood their ground and, by sheer force of personality, quietened the mob. They were applauded! There was no malice, and it really resembled a jousting act between artist and audience. Somebody had to come out on top.

When I was ten, I followed in Tommy's footsteps and managed to get a milk round in Mr Craig's Dairy. I had to start at 6.30 in the morning. My round consisted of the nearby tenements, which meant continually running up and down stone stairs. The milk was contained in elongated tin cans and, as milk was not pasteurised at this time, it was still warm. On winter mornings my hands were so cold that I would put the milk cans together and stick my hands between them. Milk jugs were left outside the front door. Emptying the cans, I always left a couple of sips in each one. After emptying a dozen cans, I had collected enough to have a decent drink! I was with Mr Craig for about six months when I was approached by a Mr Thorburn who was a bespoke boot maker. Besides doing ordinary boot and shoe repairs, he made special boots for people with deformed feet. The prowess of the man was amazing, from pieces of leather and many different sizes of shoe last, a specially made boot came into being and fitted the person it was designed for perfectly, so that he or she could walk with confidence.

He offered me a job which entailed ten minutes washing the front window in the morning and when I came home from school, sweeping up and delivering the special footwear to the people concerned. The pay would be three shillings a week. As the pay from Mr Craig was two shillings and sixpence, an extra sixpence a week awakened my entrepreneurial spirit. The big plus would be the end of being awakened at six o'clock every morning. He also said that if there were no deliveries to make, I could go on my way. It took me a split second to decide but I waited till Saturday morning. After being paid I told Mr Craig I was leaving. He was rather grim and miserly. He didn't take the news with good grace. I was subjected to a tirade about disloyalty amongst boys and the poaching by other people.

When delivering the boots or shoes to the clients, who mostly lived in well appointed houses, so were comfortably off and, to sugar the cake, quite often I would receive sixpence as a tip. I still gave Mum a shilling from my wages and, as sometimes my tips were as much as I earned, I declared that I was going to buy a new bicycle (not a second-hand one). As a new bicycle cost around four to five pounds, I had some saving to do!

As summer had started and I dearly wanted my bike before it ended, I was counting my money one evening when Mum asked how much I was short. Mum said, "The shillings that you have given me I haven't really needed them all and I wonder how many I have?" I was over the moon with delight. It did not occur to me that my dear sweet Mum was making sure I had my bike. I caught the tram to the bicycle shop and, with great aplomb, I slapped a mountain of silver coins on the counter and asked to see what he had for four pounds and ten shillings. I can still remember the colour, it was pale blue and had a front and rear lamp. It was so new and shiny, I wanted Mum and Dad to see it in its pristine condition. I walked it all the way home! Tommy reckoned I had a screw loose and whatever I did to keep it clean, the tyres would get dirty.

Mr Thorburn used to have to shut the shop on a Wednesday to take the tram to Glasgow and collect a roll of leather. It was roughly about four feet square, from the leather warehouse directly opposite the tram terminus. One day, with permission from Mum, he asked me if, after school on Wednesday, I would go into Glasgow and bring back the roll of leather? It was very easy to get to the warehouse, and then to catch the tram home and he would give me the money to pay for it. In the early Thirties, the world was a much safer place for youngsters, and a tram ride to Glasgow was an adventure, so I asked Mr Thorburn if I could bring a pal with me for company, to which he readily agreed. With Willie Pettigrew riding shotgun, we went on our way. When we got to the terminus, it was getting slightly dark as it was winter. The city noise and hubbub of voices was slightly unnerving but we soon found the warehouse, picked up the leather, paid for it and we were back in the shop before six o'clock – and proud of ourselves.

It transpired that Mr Thorburn was a devout Christian and belonged to the Methodist Church. He asked me one day if I had ever thought of joining the Boys' Brigade, a strictly Protestant youth organisation. After a discussion with Willie, we both decided to give it a try, but we found out that we had to attend Sunday School. Another discussion was required. The verdict was that we would go to Sunday School as it started at mid-day and only lasted half-an-hour. It was a few weeks before Christmas and as the Sunday School Christmas party was on a Friday evening, we decided to stick it out and have a party to go to. In idle conversation with other lads who attended the Original Secession Church in Wellmeadow Street, a much smaller church, we learned that their Sunday School was in the afternoon and being a rather chaotic affair, we registered and decided to put in an appearance the Sunday before the Christmas party. Mum was not amused but the rest of the family just put it down to Jimmy's eye for some minor scam. Christmas came and we enjoyed the parties. After a while and because of the Christian restraints the Boys' Brigade put on us, we decided to leave and to resort to our indolent ways.

In 1932, the Depression was still digging deep into the souls of the ordinary people and, to their eternal shame, the Coalition Government brought in a Means Test to ascertain whether some families were maybe getting two or three pence a week more than they could survive on. One of the bailiffs' ploys was to enter a home and if there were four people living there and there were five chairs, one was taken away. Mum and Dad told me of an instance that changed everything.

A young girl in Incle Street was learning to play on an old battered piano. The bailiffs, in their supreme wisdom, decided that it was a luxury and, as her family were on poor house relief, as the people tended to call it, they were going to confiscate it. A deep anger overcame the families around the area. On the morning that the bailiffs were due to arrive at Incle Street to extract their "booty", including the piano, the families barricaded both ends of the street, swearing that enough was enough! The bailiffs arrived and, seeing the barricade, sent for the police. The police arrived in force, under the impression that there was an unruly mob. Finding ordinary decent people deciding to stand up for whatever rights they had left, the senior policeman, on surveying the scene said, "Those people have had enough and so have we", telling the bailiffs to find some other poor soul, ordered them to leave the scene and promised the people that they would not return. The law regarding re-possession was soon changed and those human sharks disbanded.

School dinners were introduced so that needy children had at least one decent meal per day. I decided to sample it one day. When I got home, I received the biggest tongue lashing from Mum who impressed on me that the dinners were for children who needed them, not for a fat lummox like me.

Dad was now working for the Food Division in the Co-op. It involved driving a huge articulated lorry. Two days a week he delivered meat to the main meat warehouses and on the other days, it was flour, butter and sugar. As all these provisions were delivered to shops in loose form and weighed in front of the customers, the sacks that had contained the sugar Dad collected and, with the manager's permission, flayed them against the wall so that at times there was a prodigious amount of sugar that fell from them onto the clean floor. It was collected, put in a bag and distributed around the street. When Dad went to the meat market, he always managed to be given an oxtail. Mum had already bought vegetables and when he came home for something to eat, the pots were already on the stove. Mum stripped the tail of every vestige of meat and, with the vegetables soon bubbling, a wonderful smell was generated. Then Tommy or myself, whoever was first indoors, was told to chap (knock) at the doors of our neighbours and to tell them to bring their pots which were soon filled with a marvellous soup, full of goodness. Mum and Dad fed our tenement twice a week for a very long time!

Just outside Paisley Gilmour Street Railway Station, part of the sidings had fallen into disuse and the rail track had recently been ripped up. Consequently, there were huge piles of railway sleepers which were extremely thick and considered to be of no use. Dad approached the Station Master, who he knew, and offered to take them away. The Station Master agreed to this, happy to get rid of them. Dad then asked Uncle Jim Morrison if, when he was coming back from the Docks and had finished deliveries, he could use the lorry to pick up the sleepers. Uncle Jim agreed, so long as the lorry was garaged by the evening. With a gang of volunteers from the street the sleepers were soon loaded, then deposited on the waste ground near our homes. It took nearly a week sawing through the sleepers, then chopping them into pieces small enough for the fire. Fires burned in the hearths of every home in Hannah Street for a long time.

It was some time after all the timber disappeared that part of the waste ground was acquired by the Pentecostal Church, who built a 'Nissan' type large hut, inviting everybody to worship on Sunday afternoons and Wednesday evenings. Mum said they were a 'happy clappy' crowd but there was no harm in them. It was a drizzly evening one Wednesday and usually a gang of us would congregate on the stairs and swap comics and tell outlandish lies. But I decided, together with my trusty friend Willie, to pay a visit to the Pentecostal Church as we had heard that after the 'happy clappy', tea and cakes were served. That was when the trouble started. After the tea and cakes, Willie and I were asked to stay behind and, with the laying of hands, we were 'saved'. Once again, at peace with the world, I came home to an immediate slap on the behind and my Mum declaring, "That didn't save you". Once again our Christian endeavours were quickly dashed.

Dad, usually on Sunday nights, repaired our boots and shoes. Unsuspectingly, I once approached him and, opening my mouth, said I could waggle one of my front teeth. Asking to be shown it, quick as a flash, with his pliers, he pulled it out. I stood with my mouth open, not sure whether to laugh or cry. (There were no tooth fairies in those days.)

May, my eldest sister who was married, seemed to become very fat and rashly I mentioned it, to immediately get a slap on the backside. A few months later, she was in possession of a baby. (To my little mind, a woman gets fat, suddenly there is a baby and then the woman is thin again! – amazing! But one was not allowed to mention the fat bit!)

When I started writing about my family history, I had to lean heavily on what was discussed between me and primarily my Dad about worldly affairs, my dear Mum on intimate family events, and my elder brother Tommy, who is still hale and hearty and blessed, like myself, with a good memory, and my sister May, who in her ninety-sixth year, has still a very sharp mind. I visited my local library to find in-depth information regarding the depression years but all I found were cold statistics which researchers may find enlightening. But I came to the conclusion that one had to have been born into a working class family to understand, and to witness and endure the privations that families had to confront and remain intact. The rich people also suffered and, in a way, the trauma of being deprived of a very high standard of living must have been devastating. There were many suicides amongst them, yet amazingly, none to my knowledge were ever recorded amongst the working class.

I have written enough of the Depression years. Entering 1933, there was a faint whiff of optimism in the air as the keel was laid on what was to be the famous Queen Mary luxury liner. Actually the work had started long before but it was in 1933 that this leviathan started to take visible shape. The Queen Mary was in its own way a miniature town. It required the same diverse amount of services, so gradually men started to go back to work. The little non luxury shops started trading again, and even the clang from the tramcars seemed more cheerful.

In the summer months, a gang of us hiked up to the Maxwellton Braes (hills) as, not only was it one of the highest points around, it has a wonderful natural spring called "The bonnie wee well". It had a metal cup securely fastened to it so that people could take advantage of drinking from it. On our way there, we always called in at a farmhouse and, for a penny, we were given a cold drink called 'Soor Dook'. It was the residue from butter making and had a unique taste and sometimes there were specks of butter in it. (We lived well!) At the top of the 'Braes', we could see for miles and dominating the sky line was the Queen Mary, growing larger every day, till it was ready for its launch in 1934. It was a beautiful sight, the epitome of Clydeside skills. The Royal Family arrived en masse for the launching and we arrived at the top of the 'Braes' early in the morning, armed with sandwiches, a bottle of ginger beer and a blanket to sit on; it was a wonderful day. Although miles away, we could hear the sirens and the cheering as this wonderful ship slid into the water.

4 I discover girls – and war clouds gather

I HAD left Craiglea school and was now attending Mossvale, a much larger school and with greater potential for advanced subjects, such as English and Maths. It seemed I was a late learner, as I appeared to excel in these subjects and scored high marks. I also found I could draw and was picked at times to sit in parts of Paisley with imposing buildings, and to attempt to re-create them on drawing paper. I had a vivid imagination. Consequently on writing a composition on whatever subject the teacher picked, I invariably ended up with a story barely resembling the subject matter.

I left school at fifteen and entered a new establishment started by the Scottish Educational Authority, which centred on new skills necessary for the advancement of young lads just leaving school. I took a great interest in the construction industry, spending a few months in each trade. I found most enjoyment working with stonemasons, whose skill is one of the oldest in history. On the lighter side, I liked working with paints and sign writing, though not quite to the high standard required to earn a living. Anyway, I was advised it was an overcrowded profession.

At that time I started to go through the most profound awakenings of my young life. My squeals had gradually started to go deeper, and my imitations of excited girls had suddenly gone. Surprisingly Willie's voice had gone the same way! Tommy's explanation was more to the point. He said, "It's about time they dropped". Mum told him to wash his mouth out. I tried to get him to explain but he just laughed, and told me where not to be kicked in future as it would hurt, as hurt as never known before! On the subject of girls, who I had always thought to be a pain in the backside, I found myself looking as their posteriors in a completely different way, akin to enjoyment, in fact! In my generation, parents never discussed procreation of the human species and allied subjects and only hinted at it, at one's peril.

I left college (as those establishments are called now) and, being rather 'laid back' and finding nothing to worry about, I took a dead end job in a public house called the 'Hay Weighs' in King Street. Besides working behind the bar, which I quite enjoyed, and listening to the banter of the men, I learned a lot about life and the opposite sex! Bulk whisky was brought in and I helped bottling it and sticking our own labels on the bottles. I decided to sample it one afternoon but, drinking too much for my young body, I ended up inebriated and thoroughly sick. I was sent home in disgrace, lost a day's pay and was told not to come back! Mum hoped that I would finish with drink (I didn't).

Tommy was working in the India Tyre Works and, as they were working three shifts, they were looking for workers to be trained as tyre builders. Before I started work, Tommy, who being a sporty and serious type of lad who performed every task to perfection (he's been like that all his life!), and knowing my airy-fairy views of life, warned me to do my best. I certainly did my best and as the wages were very high, even after giving Mum her part of my wages, I was left, for a sixteen year old with a small fortune. I joined the Dance Academy to learn as quickly as I could as the Town Hall Ballroom was my ultimate aim – to show the girls how clever I was (or thought I was!)

To people who lived in small villages and open spaces, the grim looking tenements of dark grey stone gave the false impression that the families were dour and of a subdued nature, whereas the opposite was true. This was reflected in the clothes of the lads of sixteen and over, who went through a stage of wearing colourful clothes. I still cringe at my incursion into buying my first suit, shirt and tie. The suit was pale blue with white stripes, the shirt was white, the tie was silk in colours of the rainbow, the picture completed with yellow tan shoes.

On that first Saturday night, I emerged from the bedroom with a stupid smirk on my face, oblivious to the stupefied expressions on my Mum's and Dad's faces. Mum gasped and said, "You are not going out looking like that". Dad reckoned street lamps were not required when we were around. Our mode of dress soon palled when we realised that instead of capturing the girls, they tended to veer away from us. So the colours were laid to rest, much to Mum's relief.

I was always an avid reader, including newspapers, which made me realise that the world was becoming a dangerous place. Observations from older people made me and the lads realise that Germany was becoming dangerous and already poised to march into other countries. Being completely ignorant of the consequences of war, I felt excited at the prospect and dreamed of belonging to all sorts of glamorous regiments and of the different countries I would see.

More machines appeared in the factory. We were asked to work overtime as every factory and shipyard was soon working twenty-four hours a day on defence and armaments. But as it turned out in the end, our preparations were still woefully deficient. Dad made a very true remark, "Churchill warned the fools in 1933 that Germany was again the enemy". Some people were becoming affluent solely because of the terrible events to come.

As time went on, we tended to forget the dangers ahead and, with plenty of money in our pockets, we had a very full and entertaining week. Dancing Wednesdays and Saturdays, the cinema Tuesdays and Fridays. An ice rink had opened up in Glasgow Road, so we started to learn to ice skate, but never seemed to get the hang of it. I usually ended up with a frozen rear.

In 1936, the Paisley Council had started to build council flats with three large bedrooms and a smaller room that could be used as a bedroom, a large sitting room and a kitchen. But the greatest sight was a bathroom with hot and cold water supplied by a back boiler behind the sitting room fire, and the bonus was an inside toilet. We were in heaven! There was a front garden, and a rear for growing our own vegetables.

The flats were in large buildings, divided in two. My family had the upper floor and a Catholic family, by the name of Feeley, had the ground floor. The two families got on with each other very well. As Dad and Mr Feeley were keen gardeners, they became quite matey, and it was the same all over the estate. Privet hedges sprung up in a very short time and were lovingly clipped to a uniform size. Thinking back to our life in the tenements, we were happy there because we knew no better. But to live as we were living in our new flat was like opening a huge gate and walking away from a drab environment into a different world.

The houses were painted white and had sturdy metal gates. They overlooked a large open space where the children could play under the very eyes of the parents. By coincidence or policy, every husband had regular work, which gave the estate a sense of well being. Being seventeen, I went to bed at night thinking of girls and woke up thinking of girls. If I tried to think of anything else, the thought usually ended up thinking of a girl. Comparing today and the few years before World War II, the change in attitudes amongst the young, especially sexual, is tremendous. Our sexual awakening before the war seemed to take much longer. Perhaps because of our Presbyterian or Catholic upbringing that repressed us, a kiss and a cuddle was all that was expected, and was all that we got (if we were lucky).

The main event of the week was the Saturday night dance at the Town Hall. I still laugh at the way the girls and lads were separated. At one side of the hall were the girls and on the other side were the boys. As the band started to play, whatever dance it was, the lads had to cross over the floor and ask the girl he had chosen, "Would you like to dance?" One would think this quite a simple exercise; it was anything but simple. First, you set your beady eyes on a nice looking girl and nonchalantly start walking across the dance floor with anticipation, which soon turned to desperation, as you realised that there were several beady eyes looking at the same girl. Sometimes you were lucky and other times not! The trouble was that if you were unlucky, it meant that you were so near the other girls, the direction had to change and you had to ask the girl confronting you. If unlucky enough to have picked rather an unattractive one, you were usually told to "bugger off". If you fancied a girl and wanted to take her home, it was essential to find out how far away she lived, as I was already two miles from home and any distance in the opposite direction meant a very long walk home (it happened many times). Once I thought I had struck lucky, the girl just lived farther down from me; actually I had passed my own gate going towards her home. After a squeeze and a cuddle and feeling quite pleased with myself, I went indoors to be met with a very severe telling off. Mum said, "Didn't you know that girl is a Catholic?". I mumbled that I didn't know and made for my bed. As I lay in bed thinking back to when Tommy and I were certain Mum could read minds, I came to the conclusion that she could see through bloody curtains as well!

The sixteen/seventeen year olds had a strange sort of mating custom on a Sunday night. Paisley High Street, Causeyside Street and New Street formed a large triangle and around half-past-seven in the evening, the lads and lasses gradually started to arrive. The lasses started to walk the triangle clockwise and lads anti-clockwise. The badinage and the showing off on both sides was the main fare and usually one managed to 'click' (secure a date). The girl had to be invited to partake of an ice cream at the ice cream parlour. I used to splash out, as if I was loaded, and buy the girl a large sundae! (It cost a shilling for two).

By the end of 1938, everybody was in work except the completely infirm. Our wages had risen substantially. The unions were claiming victory for this, and it was the only time I ever heard Dad use an expletive in front of the family. He was always deeply suspicious of unions as he firmly believed that they caused more harm than good during the miners' strike and during the depression. Nevertheless, the standard of living had risen considerably and the Christmas and New Year celebrations were quite sumptuous compared with the years before, although the more serious minded were already wondering if the next festive season would be celebrated under the shadow of war. Myself and my compatriots were now old enough to understand that all our efforts in the workplace were directed to one end. Although foretold by people with vision, the efforts were already too late.

The Territorials in Paisley were the Argyll and Sutherland Highlanders and Royal Engineers, their notice boards proclaiming all the advantages of military training. Alas, our loyalties towards our local regiments did not go down very deep. The huge expanse just outside the town was turned into a naval aerodrome, together with naval personnel and living quarters, which created a small town. It is now Glasgow International Airport.

In 1939, a form of conscription was introduced for men over twenty and unmarried, ostensibly for six months but, as it turned out, most of them never left the services due to war being declared and many volunteered. With Germany massing along Poland's borders and Great Britain and France making a pact with Poland, war seemed certain.

Chamberlain's visit to Hitler was just a cruel joke and on 3rd September which was a Sunday, I was at my sister's house when an announcement on the wireless was made at noon. After the strokes of Big Ben finished, the Prime Minister Neville Chamberlain came on and, with grave tones, declared we were at war with Germany.

I kept the excitement out of my face and was prudent enough to let the grown-ups do all the talking. All sorts of preparations for war were instigated. The 'blackout' was instantly introduced, with all street lights out and curtains drawn. Some idiots seemed to think that it was all right to walk along the street with torches as big as car headlamps. They were soon disillusioned and the torches were taken off them! The Sunday night mating stroll died a death, partly because of the darkness. If you couldn't see who you are going to share an ice cream with, why take the chance,

Not far from us was the Inkerman Bowling Club of which my Dad, Bobby and Tommy were members. The Club decided that ladies could become members, so Mum was persuaded to join. In the summer evenings, it was nice to see her accompany Dad and the others to the bowling. Since we had moved, Mum found she had actually time on her hands! She even joined the local Church of Scotland, leaving the house every Sunday morning with the parting quip, "I'll be leaving you heathens to it."

5 I answer the call to arms

NOTHING seemed to happen after war was declared, or so it seemed to us, and it was known as the 'Phoney War' until the beginning of 1940. The German forces made startling advances, since known as the 'Blitzkrieg', and in May the British forces, now reaping the words of Churchill in 1933, found itself penned in on the beaches of Dunkirk. It is still one of the miracles of modern warfare that over 300, 000 soldiers, including many French, who wanted to fight on, were saved. Paisley and district became an enormous armed camp and the poor young 'civvies' found that in the dance halls especially, we were out in the cold.

1941 came and as some of the lads in the India Tyre Works were being called up, Jackie Fulton and I decided to go up to Glasgow and stick our noses into the window of the Navy Recruiting Office to see whatever there was to see. We were invited in, though told we would be called up when necessary - the Royal Marine Sergeant took my name and address. In July, I was instructed to attend the military medical centre. Obviously I had passed A1 and I received my papers to join the Royal Marines. I had never told Mum I had been to Glasgow, but Dad knew.

It was only natural when I received my calling up papers that I had mixed feelings of excitement and apprehension. I had never been further south than Edinburgh. Having to travel to Portsmouth, where the Royal Marines were stationed at Eastney Barracks, was quite an event! I had to catch an overnight train from Glasgow, and was a little surprised when Dad said that he was coming to the station with me. When we got to Central Station, he said "Let's go in for a beer". I thought to myself, "This is a first", having a drink with my Dad!

During our small talk, he casually remarked, "That little pub in

New Street will miss you and Jackie Fulton on a Saturday night, seeing both of you have been drinking in there for over a year" (under age!). We both had a good laugh about it. We finished our drinks and I went to catch the train for London. When I had found the right platform, I turned to say goodbye, and got the surprise of my life! The Dad I always thought of as the typical male Scot, never showing his feelings, had tears in his eyes. He said, "Look after yourself and do as you are told, and you will be alright. Write soon". I was glad that there were three other lads on the train bound for Eastney. We arrived in Portsmouth to find a lorry already half full of young recruits like us. On arriving we were told by a sergeant-major to form three ranks. He looked us over and remarked "I think this is going to take a bit longer than I thought". We were led into the mess hall for our midday meal. I didn't eat very much, but one of the servers remarked, "Give it a week, you will be coming back for seconds". He was right!

On Sunday morning there was a huge church parade. The duty officer shouted, "Church of England stand fast, Roman Catholics on the right, Nonconformists on the left". There were quite a few Scots like myself who were Protestants and I was elected to ask where we were to go. It was quite a big mistake, as my birth came into question, regarding my legitimacy, and I was informed that we were Nonconformists. (Never heard of the word!) We were sent to the Methodist Church, as it was the nearest to Church of Scotland in worship. There were no churchgoers amongst us, so when a W.V.S. canteen appeared just across the road from the church, there was no contest. A mug of tea and a sticky bun cost two pence, and then it was just waiting for the congregation to emerge after the service and we would wend our way back to the barracks. After a couple of Sundays, I realised that our numbers had swelled. The lure of a mug of tea and a sticky bun had taken precedence over whatever church they belonged to!

The next four weeks consisted of being fitted with our uniforms. Even in wartime, the Marines insisted on our uniforms being tailored to fit. The next item of contention was the polishing of our boots, especially the toe caps. It was the first time I came up against the term "spit and polish"; it meant precisely that! Layers of polish put on with a linen cloth and when, becoming sticky, a generous spit. A small group of us got together and generally helped each other, but we started to notice two rather aggressive lads were passing over their boots to a rather quiet lad whose bed happened to be sandwiched between them,. Very quietly, we called the lad into our inner circle, told the other two to fend for themselves, and moved his bed away from them. It was the only bullying I ever came across and as far as the lads in '40' were concerned, we were all rather happy but frustrated bullies, as we tended to retaliate.

The remaining weeks from mid September to the beginning of December 1941 involved endless square bashing and weapon training. We were eventually posted to Kingsdown on the Kent coast for our marksmen badge on the rifle range and in between times we were patrolling the coast. Just think, there was I, armed with a rifle and five rounds of ammunition, separated by the English Channel, and two million Germans! They must have been quaking in their jackboots!

In the middle of December, I was sent to a minesweeper station called the Eagle II in New Brighton, opposite Liverpool. My main duties were standing like a stuffed dummy outside the main entrance, supposedly on sentry duty. I often thought to myself, "If I ever marry and have kids and one day one of them asks me, "What did you do in the war Daddy?", the word used cannot be written! But much more was to come later. There was only one Marine near enough my own age to make friends with but his idea of a night out was two brown ales and in bed by ten, whereas I liked to go dancing. As I found out at a remarkably early age, I liked girls. He wasn't interested in signing up with me so I consoled myself that I would be going alone.

It was getting towards Christmas and I had been promised that some of the matelots and myself would get a few days leave at the New Year. One day, I came in from watch duty, cold and wet, when I noticed that on the duty board was pinned a large notice. It proclaimed: "To all Royal Marines, volunteers are required for hazardous duties". The chance to get away from this stultifying boredom was heaven sent! I immediately signed my name underneath, not bothering to look up in the dictionary what hazardous meant.

The colour sergeant informed me the next day that, as I would be on the move any time, my leave was cancelled, so I consoled myself that at least I would soon be going - where I hadn't a clue! Christmas and the New Year festivities actually were very good, and I am sorry to say that I don't remember very much. On 2nd February 1942, I was called into the Orderly Room and told to be ready to move to North Barracks in Deal to join the "hopefuls" in forming a Royal Marine Commando.

I arrived at the barracks about mid-day and I had never encountered such chaos. There seemed to be literally hundreds of marines with nowhere to go. I decided to visit the NAAFI for a mug of tea but, on seeing the crowd there, I was on the point of turning away when a rather burly lad with a Geordie accent with two mugs of tea, offered me one of them. "I got one for some other guy, but he seems to have disappeared". His name was Neil Patrick, a lad who ended up in the same platoon as myself and we fought through the entire war together.

Eventually, order prevailed and we found ourselves in a large group, and labelled X Company. A sergeant named Kruthoffer, who eventually ended up as our platoon sergeant, formed us into three ranks and informed us that we were to be marched singly in front of Captain Manners, who would either accept us and, if not accepted, to go over to a large table at the end of the parade ground, where we would be issued with a travel warrant back to where we came from!

I found myself behind Neil and as there were only a few in front of us, the wait wasn't too long before I found myself in front of Captain Manners. He said "What makes a young lad like you tired of living?". As my mind was racing, I am not sure what I said but it was in my mind to say that I did not intend to die, but I wanted to do something useful. He pointed to a clerk on the

46

other table and said that he would give me the number of the barrack room where I would be able to rest my weary bones. Neil was waiting for me and could tell by my face that I was in! However, there were many obstacles to surmount before we were accepted in the first volunteer Royal Marine Commando. There were quite a few already in the barrack room with whom I was going to serve and who became lifelong friends.

The next couple of days consisted of documentation and a very fierce medical, which left everybody exhausted. The first appearance of our Commanding Officer, Lt. Col. Picton Phillipps, was a sight to behold and his mannerisms, to many of us, were hilarious! He appeared on our first parade immaculately dressed, mounted on a beautiful white stallion, and commenced to proceed slowly down the ranks with a sergeant major at the rear. I expected him to carry a bucket, just in case! At one stage of the

Capt 'Pops' Manners showed a remarkable gift for instantly judging a man's character. Later he was promoted Lieut Col and Commander of the Commando.

proceedings, the horse's behind touched one of the lads who clearly tried to get out of the way. Picton Phillipps suddenly turned to the sergeant-major and said "Take that man's name for moving". The sergeant-major replied, "The man is a sergeant, sir". Phillipps answered, "In that case, take the man's name next to him". We knew then that we had somebody *very* different!

One piece of lunacy was that we were not allowed to leave the barracks in the evening by the main gates. We found that the only way out was by scaling an eight foot wall and we had to come back in the same way. Initiative it was called. We had another name! One of our lads was called Lofty Coles, for the simple reason that he was 6'6" tall and brawny with it. In a very short space of time, Lofty was the most popular lad in the barrack room, with free beer to boot. By cupping his hands, he launched us over the wall and with two of us remaining on the wall to help him over, we all went our merry way to the nearest pub. The only problem with Lofty was that after he had had a few beers, he tended to forget his strength and a couple of times I went straight over; luckily I didn't damage myself much. Over the next few weeks, it was very hard going as the training got tougher every day and, as it was reckoned that over 1200 Marines had volunteered, and the magic number to form the commando was under 400, the instructors were out to break us at every opportunity.

6 The tough new Commando world

ABOUT the middle of February, there suddenly appeared at the gates of the barracks, one officer and about a dozen O.R.s belonging to the Argyll & Sutherland Highlanders. They had been attached to a Royal Marine Brigade in Scotland and, having volunteered at the same time as the Marines, found themselves on their way to Deal instead of an Army depot. The first morning parades were quite amusing as Royal Marines, when they come to attention, bring their left foot smartly towards their right, barely up from the ground. Whereas, the Army bring their left foot to the right, raising it well above the ground and bringing it down with a resounding crash. At the command "Attention", there was an almighty crack, followed by a sound as if somebody had dropped something. It was only the Argyll finishing their movement. It was nine months before they were transferred to an Army Commando. One of the Argylls, Bob McAlister, like myself, married a Sandown girl and still lives in the Sandown area. There were seven '40' Commando lads who married Island girls, but sadly Bob and I are the only survivors.

It was in the last week at Deal before we left for Scotland that I made a terrible mistake that almost blew it for me. The metal in the right heel of my boot had come loose and I had to take both of them to the cobblers to be mended. I wore my best pair, which I only used for special occasions. They were quite stiff but thinking I would only be on weapon training, I was quite happy. How wrong could I be! On parade, our platoon was informed we were going on a 7-mile run and walk! I was all right for the 3½ miles but as we turned back, I was really in pain with my left foot, a blister had formed on my big toe and I was limping badly.

As with all the tough runs, a lorry stayed just behind to take any lad who had given up, subsequently to be sent back to whatever unit he had originally come from. I felt a dreaded tap on my shoulder and was told to get on the truck and report to the medical officer. My foot was cleaned up and I was told to wear a slipper for three days. The word 'devastated' was not strong enough for the way I felt when I entered the Company Office to report to Captain Manners. He was seated at his desk and said, "Heard about you wearing your fancy boots on a run and walk. Well don't worry, you won't be going anywhere, you will resume training when ready". I almost shouted with sheer joy. Crazy when you think about it! When I told the lads that I was excused all duties for at least 3 days, the language was deplorable and I told them so, adding that I would be rooting for them every morning when they left for their daily 7 mile run. I wisely shut up when I noticed 11 rifles all pointing at me!

Our commanding officer Picton Phillipps and his idiosyncrasies were a constant source of amazement. He started to prowl around in the middle of the night and to try and catch the sentries at H.Q. unawares. Incidentally, he had a room there where he slept quite often. There came the night when it was my section to do guard duty. We had already decided to keep a good look out for him in case he decided to attack one of us. Neil Patrick was on the 2.00 until 3.00 shift when he noticed a glimmer of light coming from one of the windows, and a few minutes later he heard a rustle in the bushes just behind him. Neil inadvertently struck an intruder across the shoulders and Picton, giving a yelp of pain, cried, "It's your commanding officer, carry on!" When Neil came into the guardroom, we wholeheartedly agreed with him (he was in the shit!) While on parade the next morning, a truck arrived from H.Q. with orders to pick up Neil Patrick. Neil, mouthing obscenities, boarded the truck, with all the lads promising to visit him and to look after his girl friend. He didn't think much of that!

We were all sitting around waiting for orders when Neil arrived back. With a stupid grin on his face, he said, "In future, stand up when I talk to you" and proceeded to tell us the daftest story you

Jock in July 1942, aged 20 years

ever heard. He was marched into the C.O.'s office and told to stand to attention and to wait for Picton Phillipps, who duly marched in. He stood in front of Neil, pulling back his shirt exposing a large bruise on his collar bone, exclaiming "You did this" and, turning to the R.S.M., said "For being fully alert whilst doing his duty", pointing to Neil, "I want to make this man a Lance Corporal". We only believed him when he pulled out the stripes given to him. Picton Phillipps was as daft as a halfpenny watch to many, but later he gave his life to protect his men. That was the act that we will always remember him for.

The Royal Marines Barracks were in close proximity to the town of Deal and the surrounding area for many miles was extremely built up. Consequently, the initial weeding out process was confined to the barracks' area and pounding the tarmac roads. As days went by, and especially the three days I was 'sick', I was able to watch the activities of the other companies in complete safety, without any repercussions as to why I was leading a shiftless existence whilst the others were sweating blood! I slowly came to the conclusion that my worst fears, as I was travelling down to Deal, were that my puny physique, compared to the 'Charles Atlas' types who would surely be there, would be ridiculed, and I would be sent packing. However my fear was completely unfounded. During the ensuing days, the first to drop by the wayside were the 'muscle men' as, after a couple of miles, their overdeveloped legs suffered from cramp or their lungs could not expand enough, due to too much muscle around their chest. Others lacked co-ordination in weapon training or lacked general fitness and many, realising that there was going to be very little glamour, quietly disappeared! The remaining lads, having survived so far and being formed into platoons, twenty-one in each, started to bond and help one another, something Pops Manners remarked upon, adding "There will come the day when you will depend on each other!" Therefore, the finished 'article', as our platoon officer 'Red' Whitely described him, was "lean, mean, bright-eyed and bushy tailed". By early March, every man had been assessed. The failures had been weeded out, the required 380 to make the Commando having been achieved with me being one of the idiots! We had 7 days leave and then left for Scotland for mountain training and cliff climbing.

After a tiresome journey, we eventually arrived at a small locality called Acharacle, adjacent to Loch Shiel, which would be used for sea landings from landing craft called R. Boats, and which subsequently proved to be death traps for the Canadians on the Dieppe Raid. I was in X Company and we stayed at Acharacle. The other companies were spread around the area at small localities. We were given two days to get settled in and recover from the train journey which had taken nearly twenty four hours.

There was quite a steep cliff about 50 yards from the huts and a few of us thought it would be a good idea to climb it. Once the rest of the lads had realised we were successful, everybody wanted to get in on the act. About half way up, there was a small cave that one day in the near future would come in very handy. The training was a lot tougher in many ways. For instance, we were told to go into the wilds for three days, fend for ourselves and not come back early, otherwise we would be given our ticket back to where we came from. I never realised the day would come when I would curse my own country. We were coming near the end of our stay when, in the middle of the night, we were awoken by what we thought were fireworks. In fact, the Naval Officers' Mess was going up in flames! We were told to get dressed and get on the ground. The short answer was, "Let the bastards burn". Some of our lads were detailed together with the Navy to clear the contents of the bar and cellar to a safe place, and were told not to imbibe, 'as if....

Dawn was just coming up when we were able to leave the smouldering ruins of the Officers' Mess and as I entered our room, Buzz Smith whispered to me, "We've swiped 3 bottles of whisky; where should we hide them?" We immediately called a conference and once everybody was present, Jimmy Lennen came up with the solution. The small cave half way up the cliff. As it was still semi darkness, myself and Buzz stuck the bottles inside our blouses and made for the cliff. It didn't take us long to deposit the whisky and we were back in the room in under an hour.

As we had no sleep, we were given the day off after our fire-fighting duties but were woken about ten o'clock by the Navy police and told to get outside. They were going to search our belongings, as it appeared there was booze missing and we were the prime suspects. Captain Manners, who we now called Pops, came on the scene. He told us the Navy lads had been rumbled and then turned on the police and, in disgusting language, told them to disappear. When they were gone, he said, "I hope you have hidden it well as they will be back!" and, with a grin on his face, he left. We knew then we had a good'un! It took us about a week to demolish the whisky and it tasted all the better knowing it was for free!

The following weeks consisted of long route marches and compass reading by night, nice when it was pouring with rain, which was pretty frequent. The main concern, when we were out on the moors for three to four days at a time, was feeding ourselves. However, we gradually found we were quite adept at making use of the long grass, together with a snared rabbit, which make quite a decent meal. As far as sleeping was concerned, we had one filthy blanket and by stuffing cotton in our ears to stop creepy-crawlies entering, we rolled under the nearest hedge or gorse and, believe it or not, fell asleep. However, in the morning we had to strip to the waist by a mountain stream to wash and shave. As the water was so cold, it was only when your face thawed out that you realised you had cut yourself, but by early May we were so fit, little notice was taken.

It was during a period of weapon training in the wild area, when we received an invitation to a dance! Looking around at one of the most desolate parts of Scotland, where not even a sheep or a deer was in sight, where were the girls? Laughingly telling us, one of the base matelots said "They do hold a dance once a month about 3 miles from here at a huge sheep shearing barn". "They" were the farmers and their families, drawn from an area of around 12 square miles. The dance was in two days time. It didn't start until 10 o'clock in the evening! We arrived somewhat early and watched the people roll up in pony traps, cars, vans, lorries and even on bicycles! We had a great time, hurling ourselves around like dervishes doing the Scottish dances. 'Pops' was right, I swear the few hairs on my chest disappeared after a few 'swigs' of the whisky!

It was 6 o'clock in the morning when the dance broke up and we were offered a lift back to camp. It was a good job because the landscape was like a prairie. Even if we had been driving on a six lane motorway, we would have left it many times. We laughed about it in the future and remembered the wonderful hospitality the Highlanders extended to us.

I think it was about the middle of May when we embarked on the exercise that was going to test us to the limit of our fitness. We were to travel right across Scotland from Acharacle to Dingwall with every unit, from regiments to Home Guard, against us. By marching mostly at night by compass, we evaded them, helped of course by the very nature of the country. By the fourth night, we started to get the distinct impression that we were descending and when dawn broke, we found the panorama had completely changed. The harsh stony hills and ravines had changed to a much gentler scenery. The fields were cultivated and enormous herds of cattle were grazing. We came across a large wooden building, obviously a hiker's hostel, and as it was unoccupied, we gently eased a window open and entered. On inspecting the kitchen, we found an old fashioned water pump, supplied by a well. Our Sergeant sent two lads out on a recce and when they returned, they told us that they had come across a farmhouse. Meeting the farmer's wife, they had been told that there were no 'enemy' troops in the vicinity and were invited to participate in a large bacon sandwich and a mug of tea. Before we could vent our jealousy on them, they produced a bag of tea, sugar and a can of milk! While enjoying our tea, they also said that three miles away was the main railway line from Glasgow to Inverness.

We reached the railway lines and, after about an hour, we suddenly heard the sound of a train. The first instinct was to disappear and then Kruthoffer said, "Let's stop the bloody thing, if it is not going too fast". It appeared just crawling along and as we were strung right across the track, it ground to a halt, the train driver cursing us to get out of the way. We told him we were hitching a lift and jumped aboard, filling the corridors. As the train started up, an inspector appeared, threatening to have us imprisoned, but luckily a few miles from Inverness, the train had to stop for signals. We soon disembarked and melted into the countryside. We hid in a pine forest for the remainder of the day and marched as soon as it was dark. We reached our destination mid-morning and ate a hearty breakfast.

Eventually, we were informed we were to board a converted cross-channel ferry called the "Princess Beatrix" at Invergordon and, once aboard, learned our destination was the Isle of Wight, where we were installed in civvy billets, something that at the time puzzled us. It certainly did not sink into our minds that, a second mum, a comfy bedroom and home cooking were in the offing. As it turned out, with a substantial amount of cash left over, once we had paid our weekly 'rent', we found ourselves comparatively rich! Also, I didn't realise there was a lovely redhead lying in wait for me, to whom I would return at the end of the war and marry.

We disembarked at Ryde, where we found we had a route march to Sandown. Other companies went to Shanklin and Ventnor. We were to share Sandown and Lake with A Company.

I was billeted in the Riviera Hotel with Ron Frost and Ginger Northern. Space was no problem as we had a bedroom each. Our landlady, Pearl Vanner, was an easy going lady with a happy disposition towards us. Sadly, Ginger was to die during the fighting at Dieppe and Frostie lose a leg much later on the Garigliano river. The Island was literally a heavily armed camp as, besides ourselves, there were county regiments and, significantly as far as we were concerned, the Canadians.

The type of training we engaged in with the Canadians, involved the use of their assault courses, and practice assault landings from the sea. Portsmouth Docks were a favourite area for street fighting, much to the annoyance of the dockers and naval staff. It became obvious to us that we and the Canadians were being trained together for something very big. Although we were young (average age 19), we all got on very well with our landladies who, in turn, more or less adopted us. So much so, that if we had a very strenuous day ahead of us, we were warned not to stay out to all hours - if we did, we were told off!

An early picture of Molly and me. We met when we were stationed at Sandown. At that time I little thought that she was to be my life partner.

Around 7th July, we were transported to Ryde Pier where we went aboard *HMS Locust*, an old and dispensable gunboat from the China Seas, and realised that the 'something big' was really on! For two days we had been incarcerated in Upper Chine School at Shanklin, supposedly for security reasons. The upshot of this was the spectacle of hordes of girlfriends hanging over the walls, with the lads hanging out of the windows having animated conversations, as the military police had given up (female power).

No sooner had we boarded the *Locust* when orders were reversed and we were taken off, went back to our billets and there given twelve days leave. After leave, we were soon back to rigorous training with explosives, which seemed to indicate the direction in which we were going to be employed.

The Duke of Cornwall Light Infantry were stationed in Sandown Barracks. They disliked us (actually, they hated us!). The reasons were fairly straightforward. We had a lovely life in billets, looked after and practically tucked into bed at night. Together with our extra pay and money left over from our billet allowance, we were quite rich compared with the D.C.L.I. The other big plus was that we were young and most of us very handsome (!!) and had egos as big as houses. It all came to a head one night outside the Manor House Dance Hall where we had one almighty fight, inside and out. The place was shut for a week.

I had just started to go out with Molly and had agreed to see her in the dance hall. After the fighting had finished, I spied her going up Lake Hill on her way home. I tried to tidy myself up as I reached her, full of excuses but, sadly, I did not make much of an impression. Enough to say, I did not know she could swear so nicely; all her anger directed at me. My romance was finished.

7 The disastrous Dieppe raid

COME 17th August and the idea that it was going to be just an ordinary day was soon to be forgotten. We were ordered to assemble at the rear of the Belgrave Hotel in Sandown. There we found ourselves priming grenades, filling Bren gun magazines and checking our guns. The explanation given was that we were going on an exercise! Even the dimmest amongst us wasn't going to buy that.

Pops Manners was quite serious when he told us we were not to repeat anything that had gone on that day. I remember going back to our billet where we automatically started to get our equipment up to scratch, our weapons cleaned and oiled. We didn't go out that evening, adding to Pearl Vanner's suspicion that

Chasseurs *of the Free French Navy formed part of* HMS Locust's *escort on the approach to Dieppe*

something was up or that, much less likely, we were becoming quite responsible in our behaviour. We paraded quite late on the morning of the 18th to give us time to get our equipment in order, and in late afternoon we boarded lorries to take us to Ryde Pier Head and, lo! and behold, there was the *HMS Locust* moored just off the Pier. We soon boarded, with part of A Company. It was so crowded that anybody who had grenades hanging from their pouches were told to f… off, as we did not want any accidents amongst ourselves.

There was quite an armada of fighting ships crammed into the Solent and all set sail just before midnight. The few hours beforehand were spent being told that our destination was Dieppe and our task was to demolish the German Naval Headquarters and sink every boat in sight. However, as the *Locust* was destined to ram any obstacle in its way, it was obvious that it was not coming back. Somebody tentatively asked, "How do we get back?" It was a question that should not have been asked and there was just a stony silence. Later it was suggested in a jocular tone, "Why don't we raise one of the boats that we have just sunk, dry it out, find out from the Germans where they kept the diesel and fill up?" That too, was greeted by a stony silence.

It was about three o'clock in the morning, still dark, when suddenly the sky erupted to our left! We learnt later that No. 3 Commando had unluckily sailed straight into a small German coastal convoy, and was so reduced that it could not achieve its objective.

As we became the leading craft approaching the dock gates, it seemed as though all the enemy weapons were trained on us. Guns either side of the entrance opened up and we received two direct hits. There were many casualties and, sadly, Ginger Northern was killed and 'Pusser' Hill lost his left leg. There were minor wounds amongst many, especially the navy lads. As there was very little protection on the deck, we dreaded the next salvo, but luckily the *Locust* was still afloat. The skipper had already put her full astern and kept going till we were just out of range – for the time being.

It was still dark but, looking over towards the beach where the Canadians were landing, it was a complete inferno. All we could see and hear were explosions, tracer bullets and screams. Some of the landing craft, which were partly wooden hull *Eureka* boats, had become death traps and were burning fiercely. Of the Tank Landing Craft some were badly hit and had begun to sink.

At first light a Motor Landing Craft came alongside containing our commanding officer Lt. Col. Picton Phillipps and most of headquarters. He ordered everybody to join him. Most of us managed to scramble aboard his craft when suddenly a couple of shells landed not far from us. The skipper of the *Locust* immediately set us adrift, leaving quite a few of our lads still aboard. As we started going in, the C.O. told us we were going to land on White Beach to assist the Canadians who were in dire straits.

As we neared the beach, we were hit directly on the ramp, which caused the landing craft to go broadside on but luckily it righted itself. We grounded on a sand bank about six yards from the beach which, incidentally, consisted of large pebbles. Any tank which managed to land became so embedded that they could not move and became, like us, sitting targets. We were soon the centre of attention and the skipper of the landing craft, desperate to get rid of us, tried to lower the ramp and finding it jammed, climbed up with a hammer. As soon as he showed himself, he fell dead amongst us. Jock Alexander acquired a Bren gun and with me acting as No. 2, started to fire at the top of the cliff, doing some damage. Tragically, he was shot in the head. The Bren fell into the water.

The Colonel realising the hopelessness of the situation, climbed on an ammunition box and, with Captain Comyn holding onto his legs as the boat was rocking heavily, put on white gloves so that the other incoming craft would see him, and signalled them to turn back. Within seconds, he and the Captain were cut down in a hail of bullets. Nevertheless, our second in command, Major Houghton, had already landed. Everybody was doing their best to return fire at obvious targets but by then we knew it was a

A destroyer picks up survivors from a crippled landing craft. I was plucked from the sea on the end of a rope.

useless exercise. We were hit again at the rear, killing the navy lads and wounding two of our own. A fire started which, at the time, seemed to seal our fate, but the Regimental Sergeant Major, a really tough chap, ordered the ones nearest the ammunition to start throwing it overboard. We would have been blown to bits if the flames had reached it. That accomplished, we managed to get the wounded up towards the front and he turned to us and yelled "I'm afraid it is every man for himself, try and make it back". To this day, I give thanks for the vigorous training we had endured as nobody panicked, helping each other to get rid of our equipment and throwing ourselves over the side, two at a time so that we would not finish up in a large bunch. We had taken our boots and blouses off. I kept my trousers on, as many did, in case we had to turn back and give ourselves up. Quite a few, not good swimmers, decided to take their chances on the beach which by then was hell on earth. Men were hugging the cliff face, and the dead were lying with hardly a space between them. As far as I was concerned, there was only one choice – take one helluva chance before giving up – to swim for it. I almost fell on top of one of the platoon officers, Johnny Overs, who asked me what I was going to do, but before I could reply he just sighed and sank into the water. He had been shot in the head.

I swam away as strongly as I could; the fear that I could feel within me almost made me sick. We gradually got within touching distance of each other. I found myself teaming up with Freddie Usher who shouted, "I reckon swimming the Channel will be no worse than what we have just left". I know it is a strange thing to remember but it was a beautiful sunny day. This must have helped us to stave off the cold for our long immersion. As time went by, sometimes holding our hands over our heads to protect ourselves from shrapnel dust – minute particles that stung quite sharply – we began to feel despondent, as the naval craft kept sweeping up and down the waves, making us choke.

One odd incident happened when a pilot and a parachute landed amongst us quite far out. We tore the parachute away from his face to find he was German. As we had been in the water for over two hours, we were not much interested in him and told him he could make for the shore. He replied, "I would end up dead if I did that. Do you mind if I join you?"

Eventually, a flak ship came slowly up to us and shouted, "Next time around, we will slow down and throw ladders and rope over the side. Grab when you can as we can't stop". There were about ten of us. We got into some form of straight line and, frantically rubbing our hands to get some feeling in them, waited for the ship to turn and come back. It slowed down and a rain of rope ladders and just ordinary rope came flying over the side and everybody lunged for one. As I had very little feeling in my hands I twisted the rope around my wrists and two navy lads pulled me up. Full of concern, they enquired as to what I was and on replying I was a marine, their faces changed to distaste and one said, "Bloody marines get everywhere" but helped me down below to strip and dry myself and have a wonderful mug of hot cocoa.

As my body began to warm up, I realised that the back of my legs were very sore. Due to the chaffing of my trouser legs and the sea water, they were quite raw, so one of the navy medics slapped some cream on them. Fred and I were each thrown an old pullover, trousers and a pair of boots with no laces, which we accepted thankfully.

About an hour later, Fred came over to me and said, "I have just volunteered both of us to take over an Oerliken as quite a few Marines have become casualties". (The gun crews were Royal Marines). I replied, "For the size of you, Fred, you have one helluva big mouth". We got up onto the gun deck and the navy gunnery officer said, "Keeping the gun trained on top of the cliffs will help the lads trapped on the beach". Although we only lasted half an hour at the most, I felt we had done something positive and as the ship turned for home, the skipper shouted, "Well done, bootnecks", we felt included in the praise. It was dark before we docked at Newhaven. We were ordered onto the quayside and dispersed among the numerous huts, in case of 'Jerry' air attacks.

In the morning our R.S.M. came round and told us breakfast was being served in the navy mess hall. When we were finished, trucks took us to a Canadian camp for de-briefing. There were separate tables and we just picked one. A Canadian officer sat down opposite. All he wanted to know was the names of men I knew for certain had been killed. When I had given him this information, he shook my hand and said, "Thank you, Royal, and next time it's got to be better". We were given coffee laced with a large dollop of rum, which made our heads spin. We were then put on lorries to take us to the Portsmouth Isle of Wight ferry. When we embarked we all made for the lounge bar. Half way down the steps, I accidentally tripped but was caught by a naval petty officer. He said I looked a right comical sight and I was in dire need of a large whisky, which he duly bought me. He told me he had just come off a flak ship that had rescued more of our lads. Back at Sandown railway station, we were told to go to our billets and get cleaned up, then to report to Company office for pay. Making our way back I noticed quite a few landladies standing at

A German photo of one of our tanks, knocked out on the beach amid bodies of fallen soldiers.

different corners. I can still clearly remember the strained expressions on their faces, looking for their own lads. I was nearly back at my billet when I saw Jock Alexander's landlady. I went over to her and told her that Jock was dead. When I saw the look on her face, I was overcome with emotion myself and I can't recall what was said between us as we parted company.

I realised I had my own landlady to confront and as I went through the front door, Pearl embraced me and asked when the other two were coming. I told her Frosty shouldn't be long but Ginger was dead. She said that when Frosty came in she would make us something to eat. In the meantime she would make some tea and then went into the kitchen. I could hear her crying so I thought it best to leave her alone. Frosty came in a few minutes later and I told him that Pearl knew about Ginger. He was glad I had to be the unlucky one to tell her and, almost as an afterthought, said, "Free beer in the Castle tonight so we had better be early to get in front of those other thirsty b……s"

We both got cleaned up and changed, sat on our beds, and it was then that the whole enormity of the last two days hit us and we felt overcome with a sudden weariness. Pearl shouted for us to come down for something to eat. By now she was fully composed and full of concern when I told her I had to report to the army doctor at the barracks so I could have my legs seen to. She insisted on seeing the damage so, without embarrassment, I dropped my trousers.

We got down to the Castle just after seven and just managed to get a free pint before the other thirsty b……s came in. Ted Barber, the landlord, had laid on sandwiches so the evening went well and the tensions that everybody felt gradually eased.

That night it was a remark made by Willie McKnight to Dick McConkey that had everybody in stitches. It appears that during the carnage, on the order to abandon the landing craft they were both on, Willie declared that he could not swim but he didn't want to be taken prisoner. So Dick said that if he managed to get him back, Willie would owe him ten shillings. With the help of Charlie Betts, they had tied two life jackets around him and giving him one to hold, then literally threw him over the side. They reckon he almost bounced hitting the water. Finding an old scaling ladder, they got him onto it and promptly swam towards England. Willie now said to Dick, "I suppose you still want my hard earned ten shillings?" Dick retorted that he was the one who had found it hard but made a concession that they would drink it between them! Incidentally, Mr Bolwell, who owned the Manor House Dance Hall, gave the entire Commando a free dinner inside the dance hall, including a ticket which entitled each of us to one whisky and two pints of beer.

The day before we went on leave, I was still pretty sore and as I was hobbling up Sandown High Street, Molly came out of the shop she worked in and asked how I was, remarking that I wouldn't be dancing for a while, but there was a good picture on at the Queens tonight, if I wanted to go. The romance was on again!

To explain the mutual warm feelings existing between our landladies and ourselves, it was obvious that they became our surrogate mothers. They scolded us if we left things lying around. I will always remember the first order our landlady gave Ginger, Frosty and me as we presented ourselves at the front door. "There will be no cleaning of weapons on the carpet, in the front room or in the bedrooms." Pearl let it be known that our choice of girlfriends left a lot to be desired, but one day, she called me into the kitchen and said, "I saw you with Molly Cooper the other day. You must know she is a very nice girl and you should behave yourself". I replied that I certainly knew she was a very nice girl as I had bruises to prove it! She didn't think much of that remark!

It was during the 'Ice Age' period between Molly and myself that a few of us started to hang about the W.A.A.F. quarters at Yaverland and were creeping into our billets rather late. I was much later than usual one night and, rather than use the front door which made a loud noise on opening and shutting, I elected to climb through the kitchen window. I found myself stretched across the kitchen sink and a few inches from the floor when suddenly the light was switched on. Pearl was standing in all her glory with about twenty yards of ribbon in her hair and exclaiming, "Do you know the time?" I felt like saying that that was precisely why I was climbing in through the window. While making me a cup of tea, I was thoroughly taken to task for my behaviour. Then she delivered the marvellous punch line: "A boy of your age should not be behaving like this so I am going to write to your mother who, I hope, will put you right." Keeping a straight face, I accepted the mug of tea and made my way to my room. I told Frosty the next morning to mend his ways or his mum would be informed. Seriously, we knew she was only looking after us in a loving way.

A few days after the raid, a German plane came over the Sandown area and dropped a load of leaflets showing a lot of prisoners being marched along the streets of Dieppe. One of the lads was clearly recognisable as John Taylor who lived in Paisley. I didn't know him very well as he was billeted in Ventnor. When the

The propaganda leaflet scattered by plane over Shanklin. It showed many pictures of our captured comrades being marched away from the town to prisoner of war camps. Mocking our efforts, it was entitled 'We (meaning the Canadians) and the British invade France'

news came through that two of our lads had won the Military Medal, well deserved as they both had done sterling work with the Bren gun, I felt very sorry for Jock Alexander who also did sterling work with the Bren and obviously was doing some damage to have been singled out to be shot through the head.

As I went through the war and witnessed many brave acts that earned no official recognition, we all realised that you have to be in the right place at the right time and to be seen by the right person.

After Dieppe, much was made of the 'valuable lessons that had been learned'. However, the Canadians, who bore the brunt of the aborted attempts to capture the town, were bitter about the loss of so many of their men.

For us, this baptism of fire, taught us the difference between 'play soldiering' on countless training exercises and the stark reality of the horrors of live action. Dieppe was a grim lesson. We learned much later that of the 6000 men who had taken part in this disastrous adventure, a total of 3560 were dead, wounded or taken prisoner of which 3300 were Canadian soldiers.

Pops Manners was promoted to Commanding Officer in succession to Lt. Col. Picton Phillipps and gave the survivors of the horror which was Dieppe ten days leave. When I got home, Mum said that Mrs. Taylor had been to visit her as she had not heard from John. When I produced the German photograph, I decided to go and visit her. When she opened the door, she almost fainted as she was sure that John had not survived. However, as I quickly showed her the photo and she recognised him, a wave of relief came over her. I stayed about an hour and she became happy enough to realise that though it might take a long time, at least he would be coming home. My legs healed fairly quickly and I didn't bother going to the Military Hospital, as I should have done. Needless to say, I didn't spend much money in the pubs as I was feted as some form of celebrity. I felt for Mum and Dad when my leave was up and I got ready to return. I guessed how they were feeling. The awful truth was I couldn't wait to get back to the good life and Molly!

8 A quiet interlude and love finds a way

DURING September, there were many changes to the structure of the Commando. Companies were changed into Troops which were smaller in structure, consequently A, B, D, H.Q. Companies became A, B, P, Q, X, Y, H.Q. Troops, which meant with the same structure of three Platoons to a Troop, Officers, and N.C.O.'s significantly almost doubled our fire power. Our reinforcements arrived after very hard training at the Commando training camp. They soon jelled with the rest of us and some still survive as good friends to this day.

Our Troop Commander Captain Neil Maude seemed hell bent on the lads becoming demolition experts. One day, under the leadership of our platoon officer, Lieutenant Dai Morgan, we approached a large rusty, metal tank embedded in the sand on Shanklin beach, with the express purpose of lifting it clear of the beach by using explosives. Pops Manners had given permission as the properties opposite were either empty or had been bombed. With a lot of cursing, huffing and puffing, we eventually got underneath the tank to enable the explosives to be packed.

While Neil Maude set the fuses, we retreated about 200 yards towards the pier (extra protection). There was a terrific explosion, accompanied by about two tons of sand reaching for the sky with the tank in the middle of it. We watched its descent with morbid fascination. Would it land on the beach, in the sea or end up going through the roof of one of the houses? With more luck than judgement, it landed on the beach. Pops Manner's laconic remark was, "I think rather less pepper in the soup next time!" We spent the rest of the day sweeping up the promenade and depositing the sand back on the beach. That evening we decided that, while hugging our pints in the Castle, next time the word 'demolition' was mentioned, we would not be around!

At the end of the promenade was Shanklin Chine which was, and in essence still is, a deep ravine with steep sides and at the landward end was a waterfall. We used it for cliff climbing and by stretching a rope from side to side across the ravine, we crawled across. It was aptly named the 'cat walk' and if anybody got up to mischief, they found themselves climbing the waterfall. I can assure you it was a very cold and wet experience.

In early October, we left the Island and arrived in Weymouth where we had to find our own billets. We were there for about a month and on my birthday, the 26th, we were issued with the Green Beret, which was to become famous during the war. With other specialist troops around us, it was evident that some form of expedition was on the cards, but eventually this was discarded, because of careless talk amongst certain people, who should have known better. At the end of October, we prepared to move back to the Island – to our great delight – and, typical of Pops Manners, he decided that we should march there!

It was raining when we first set off, but the sun came out at mid-day when we started to get very hot, and were grateful for a ten-minute break every two hours. It was early evening before we reached a small village – I don't remember the name. We were ushered into the village hall and the wonderful Women's Institute ladies had a meal ready for us. Pops announced that the second half would start at 6 a.m. next morning and wouldn't finish until we got to Lymington. As our feet were not only tired but also very hot, we took our boots off. Shortly afterwards we were told that we could visit the two pubs in the village and that the maximum we were to drink was two pints. We had to arrange to go in relays so that we would not crowd the locals. When it came to our section's turn to go down to the pub, Buzz Smith, looking down at his feet, declared, "I am going down in my socks. I am not wearing those bloody boots". We all thought it a good idea and arrived in the bar in just our socks. The locals thought it was hilarious and one old lad shouted, "They were bleeding right, whoever said that all commandos had a screw loose". Ronnie

Foster asked if he had any objection to us buying him a pint. He had none whatsoever! We were off on the march by 6 o'clock in the morning and arrived at Lymington in the early evening, boarded the car ferry and gave a cheer when Pops Manners said that there would be lorries waiting to take us to our respective billets. Our landlady, Pearl, gave Frosty and me a big hug and for the life of me I can't remember what we had to eat, but within the hour we had had a bath and were supporting the bar at the Castle with the usual drunkards.

Our new platoon officer, Dai Morgan, proved to be a good lad in every way but we found out to our cost one day that we could try his patience once too often. We were marching along the Sandown sea front and were told repeatedly to stop talking. As this order was unsuccessful, he made us 'about turn' near the Battery Gardens and march along the sea front until we got to the pier, which incidentally was split in two as an anti-invasion measure. He gave the order "Left wheel" and we found ourselves marching towards this chasm and the false comfort, that he would order "About turn" or at least "Halt", didn't come. So we all marched in threes straight into the sea. To make sure that we did not fall on top of each other, we had to mark time, standing still for a few seconds before the next three went over. When we dragged ourselves out of the water, we were made to form up again and carry on marching, with the order, "No talking, please". Mid-day, we presented ourselves at the kitchen door of our billet, knowing that to walk through the hallway in the damp state we were in would have brought heavy recriminations from Pearl. She made us strip in the shed, giving us dry clothes before letting us into the dining room. We thankfully sat down to a large plate of hot soup. Pearl shook her head and said, "I give up. It is like looking after a pair of daft pups".

When we think of discipline, it usually meant obeying every order our seniors gave, but quite often it did not seem to apply to us. Pops Manners, giving his ruling on some 'ill disciplined' acts, said that because of the type of training ingrained into us - to be independent-minded - it would be natural there would sometimes be a collision of wills. For example, Dai Morgan decided that we would take a blanket with us and sleep under the stars on the Downs just outside Brading, as we were getting too used to our comfortable beds. We arrived at our allotted place, lit a fire and one bright lad suggested that we have a singsong, and he was quickly told where to go! As we tried to make ourselves comfortable, we noticed that Dai Morgan had a very comfortable sleeping bag. On making it known that we envied this desirable piece of kit, he made a very unfortunate remark, "What are you going to do about it?" It was nearly midnight before we were sure that he was fast asleep and then we quietly picked up our gear and went back to our billets, leaving him on his own. As we paraded next morning, we all wondered what he would be cooking up for us, and we soon found out. Full fighting order and weapons and an 8 mile run and walk, starting from Sandown to Apse Heath, left to Whiteley Bank, onto Shanklin and back to Sandown. His trump card was that he rode a bike all the way!

We always paraded outside our billet in the mornings. One day, as our sergeant was shouting the roll call, he eventually came to Frosty and receiving no answer, repeated himself. A window shot up and Frosty, leaning out said, "I'll be down in a minute" and promptly shut the window. Sarge then carried on with the roll call. Frosty eventually appeared and nothing was said. Discipline was very strict when it mattered, other times it was hilarious.

The rest of the year was quiet and Christmas came and went with Molly and me being quite content to be in each other's company.

By the end of March 1943, we were in no doubt that we were on the move. We returned to Scotland in early April to the Ayrshire coast, where our training consisted of weapon training and exercises lasting two and three days at a time. At the end of April, we moved into civvy billets in Kilmarnock. Our new family was very nice and, as Frosty had become batman to our platoon officer, I teamed up with Ronnie Foster. One day Ronnie and I found ourselves in front of our Troop Commander who said, "It appears that both of you have volunteered to take charge of a new weapon called the Bangalore torpedo which blows up barbed wire on the beaches and gun emplacements". Ronnie replied, "As we have volunteered, just what the hell are they?" We made our way to the weapons store and found that they were long metal pipes about five feet long, filled with explosives, set off with a twenty second pencil fuse which was crushed to set it off. We went back to Captain Maude and enquired if there was to be extra danger money. His reply is unprintable!

Early in June, we embarked on the troop ship *Derbyshire* to do a landing on the Isle of Arran at night and it lasted till morning. During the exercise, Ronnie and I were presented with the new "secret" weapon and, as we made our way inland, we were confronted by a dummy gun emplacement. With the rest of the platoon firing over our heads, we stuck this lethal piece of pipe into the barbed wire, banged the fuse, and ran for our lives. It was a good job we had moved as fast as we could. We were barely flat on the ground before there was one almighty explosion, and we were covered with earth, rock and pieces of barbed wire. As the rest of the platoon had been caught up in the mayhem, they had the gall to blame us for having to pick all sorts of rubbish from their ears and from down their shirts! We re-embarked on the *Derbyshire*, were slung off at Greenock, and made our way back to Kilmarnock to our billet.

Kilmarnock was only a few miles from Ayr which housed a very popular racetrack and our troop commander, Neil Maude, was a betting man. As there were no licensed betting shops in those days, a back street bookie had to be found. There was no better person to ask than Dick McConkey, our intrepid hero who saved Willie McKnight from a watery grave at Dieppe but which cost Willie ten shillings in the process. A bookie was found and a bet was placed on behalf of Neil Maude. Dick was to return the next day if there were any winnings. Later that evening, the good news was that Neil Maude's horse had come in first and the winnings were over £1, which was quite a lot of money in 1943, and which Dick was briefed to collect in the morning. Before midday, he cleared off and collected the winnings. Trying to put himself into the best light possible, Dick told us of the events following. "I was just passing the 'Blue Boar' when I heard the sliding of bolts and a key turning! I decided that a couple of pints would do no harm, but then time became rather a blur!" Minutes before the 2.30 p.m. parade, a figure appeared, drunk as a skunk. Realising this within seconds of going on parade, we pushed him into the centre rank with the forlorn hope that he wouldn't be noticed, but as open order march was given by Sgt. Russell who had just appeared, Dick collapsed in a heap. Neil Maude arrived and marching up to the 'heap' lying on the ground prodded him with his boot and said: "Where is my bloody money?" As you can guess, there was no reply and we were told to get rid of him. The upshot was that Neil Maude deprived Dick of six shillings every pay day for four weeks. It cost Dick slightly more than the winnings, but we persuaded him to forget it as he was lucky to get away with it so lightly. Life in X Troop was never dull.

It was not very far from Kilmarnock to Paisley, my hometown. By an amazing stroke of good fortune, my Dad still worked for the Paisley Co-operative. He drove a huge lorry and trailer through the night to the Kilmarnock Milk Depot and, when loaded with milk, drove back to Paisley. I was given permission, as long as there were no exercises during the weekend, to go with Dad, and usually with Ronnie Foster and Happy Day, on the truck back to Paisley. We arrived at our home around 8 o'clock on Saturday morning, just in time for breakfast. Mum always saw to our needs with a huge smile on her face. Whenever she spoke to the neighbours, it was always, "My boys are back for the weekend".

Saturday night was always pub night with Dad. One night, it coincided with my youngest sister's birthday. We hired a hall and an accordion player and with plentiful "carry outs" of whisky and beer, and the noise gradually getting louder and louder, we all had a marvellous time! We always caught the day shift lorry on Sunday afternoon back to Kilmarnock.

I am sure it was a Monday around the middle of June when we were told that we were given four days' leave, told to write in our travel warrants, and go. I was beset with a conflict of emotions.

Should I go home for the four days, or go and see Molly. I argued with myself that I saw my family nearly every weekend and, with a bit of luck, I would be back on the Friday and I could see them then. My mind was immediately made up when Neil Patrick and Charlie Betts, who were already engaged to their girl friends, said that they were going to try and get onto the Island to spend the days with them. As the Island was a prohibited area, the chances were that we would not be allowed on. We approached Ken Morris, who was the Orderly Sergeant, who told us that we definitely could not get on but made our warrants out for Portsmouth Harbour and said, "It is only a little stretch of water stopping you".

We arrived at Portsmouth Harbour. By the gangway onto the ferry was a lone naval policeman. There was no point in hanging about and so we approached him, presenting our travel warrants which, of course, ended at the Harbour. We immediately entered into our sob story that the girls we were engaged to lived on the Island and we only had four days' leave. We were taking a chance that we would be allowed to go over. He studied us for a few moments and then told us we had better buy our tickets while he went to the toilet. He added a rather ominous note when he said, "It is Air Force policemen at Ryde Harbour and it would make their day to send you lot back!"

As we had come this far, we decided to try and make it to Sandown. As we neared Ryde Pierhead, the plan was to let all the passengers off the ferry and then make a run for it, praying that the Sandown train would be in, then to squeeze under the seats, hoping there would be enough room. As there were three platforms in those days and always trains there, we hoped the R.A.F. wouldn't know where to look first. As the last passenger left the ferry and as others started to come aboard, we charged down the gangway, dodged through the people, got into separate compartments and managed to hide under the seats. We heard quite a bit of shouting and were really glad when the porter shut the carriage doors and the train was on the move. When we got off at Sandown, it turned out that Neil and I were lucky enough to start off with empty carriages, but two people got into Charlie's compartment. He said their faces were a study when he looked out from underneath the seat. He told them he would explain later, once the train got on its way.

I stayed with Pearl Vanner and by keeping a low profile, Molly and I enjoyed each other's company for three days. During our illicit escapade on the Island, at times we met with other landladies and we learnt that they missed us very much. No. 5 Army Commando had taken our place and I am sure their lads were no better or worse than we were, but I think the length of time we stayed with them and our being their first 'lodgers' casualties created a special niche in their hearts. 46 R.M. Commando followed No. 5 Army, who much later had a stone plaque inserted into one of the entrance piers of Upper Chine School.

Because of the easy living conditions and meeting Molly, we had a great fondness for the Island and its people. Whereas Charlie and Neil being engaged were convinced they would be returning, Molly and I could only promise to write. Not knowing what the future held, a promise was all that could be made. In conversation with Pearl, she said she had no wish to take in any of No. 5 Commando, the main reasons being that she had become too fond of us. When Ginger was killed at Dieppe, she realised that the lad had two mothers grieving for him. "In the main, No. 5 were much older than you were and if they did not behave as they should, how would I react? Besides feeding you, once your daily training had finished I felt I was the one looking after you, including all your private thoughts, of which girls took up 80% of your time, so when you and Frosty finally left, I sorely missed the noise and the laughter, so I just shut the doors".

Our leave was soon over and as we approached the R.A.F. at Ryde Pier, we told them that we were on embarkation leave and they could not detain us. They told us that when we rejoined our unit, there would be severe punishment for entering a prohibited area and they would be sending on all the necessary documents. A few days after we were back, we were summoned to appear

JOCK'S TRAVELS
with
40 RM Commando
after Dieppe

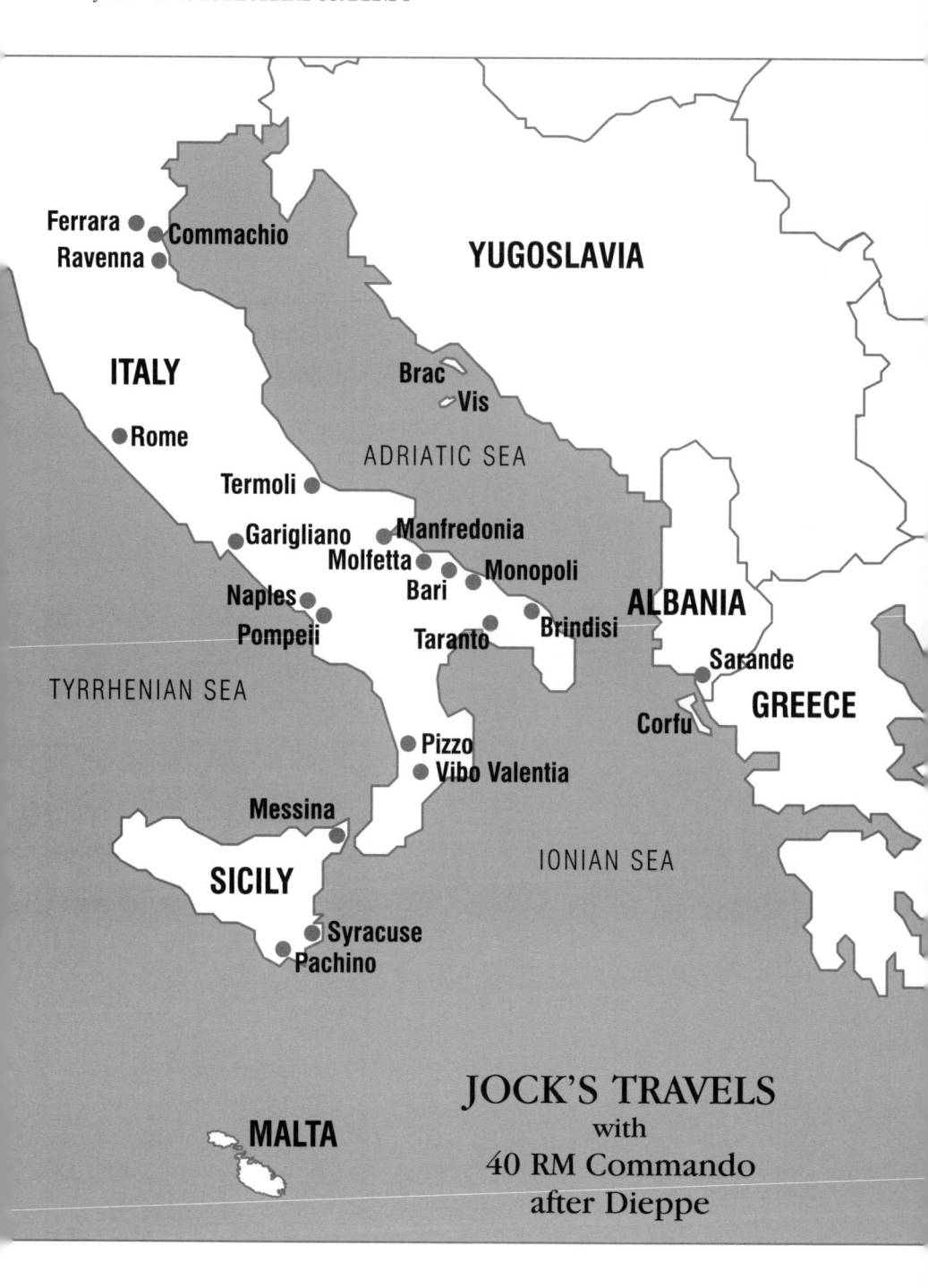

before Pops Manners. Standing in front of him, he said, "I have a document from the Military Police stating that you had entered a prohibited area without permission, namely the Isle of Wight. Explanation, please?" We told him the complete story, including diving under the seats. A smile appeared on his face and he declared that great initiative had been shown. He tore up the papers, throwing them in the bin, and told us to clear off.

The idea that I would be able to see Mum and Dad was soon scuppered as we heard the news that we were waiting for. We were told to get rid of all unnecessary gear and that we were on our way. I think it took at least a couple of days before the entire Commando was on board the *Derbyshire*. Then as the Canadians started to come on board, coupling up with the *Princess Emma*, with more Canadians and 41 R.M. Commando, we realised our war was just starting.

9 The Sicily mission

THE TROOPSHIP was packed to the gunnels and eventually we were allotted our small part of the ship, given hammocks and for some time tried to tie them properly, which was hilarious. Considering the close proximity of every hammock, it was a good job we had all been properly introduced. We were lucky with the weather and the horror stories about the Bay of Biscay didn't come to anything. The washing facilities were truly dreadful and to try and get a lather from salt water soap was impossible. The long trough where we washed became so crowded that you had to be careful it was your own face that was being washed and not somebody else's! The food was awful but, as we were always hungry, we didn't bother asking what it was - it just disappeared down our throats.

I believe it was on the third day out that we were told that Sicily was to be invaded and 40 and 41 Commando were to be the first to land and form a bridgehead for the Canadians. Maps of the Sicilian coastline appeared and we spent every day studying them and our allotted tasks. One morning, having been given our Bangalore torpedoes and making sure we had the proper detonators, we presented ourselves to the Canadians, explaining fully what they were and that our individual task was to make sure the beaches were clear of any obstacles. The senior Canadian officer made us feel very proud when he said, "40 Commando served us well at Dieppe and I know you will do so again".

Intense weapon training continued, we studied maps until it became second nature, when suddenly asked a question, for the correct answer to just roll off your tongue. As Pops Manners declared, "We fail, it all fails". We realised what a great responsibility rested on our shoulders. It still filled us with awe every time we looked around at the enormous size of the convoy. It seemed to the naked eye that the line of ships was endless. Destroyers darting among us, we all knew were our only defence against submarines!

One afternoon, it was announced that in future no rubbish was to be thrown overboard and noise was to be kept to an absolute minimum. The reason was that we were nearing the Straits of Gibraltar which are quite narrow, and we had to get through into the Mediterranean Sea as quickly and as quietly as possible!

On 9th July 1943 we were ordered to don our equipment and make our way to our allotted L.C.A.'s and settle down as best we could. Considering the hundreds of troops aboard, there was no confusion and we were allowed to loosen our straps, and a huge canteen (it could have been tea, or might have been coffee) appeared. It was greeted with thanks.

Just after midnight the L.C.A.'s started up. Almost at the same time, the sky suddenly came alive with bright orange flashes from the battleships and heavy cruisers farther out to sea from us. You could feel the displacement of air as the huge shells screamed past us on their way to the beaches, combined with the racket of the bombers dropping their load. It was the most lethal fireworks' display we had ever seen. Frosty, who was next to me, made a very true remark: "Only half of this and Dieppe would have been a different story". Although we were about 3 miles from the shore of Sicily, it was clearly visible, illuminated by the explosions and flares.

We were soon lowered and hit the water with a thump. We took our positions amongst the other assault craft and were on our way. My feelings were an awful mixture of fear and excitement which, later on, I learnt was shared by everybody. The destroyers were racing up and down behind, firing with everything they had, making the air crackle, and my eardrums ache.

As we hit the beach at Pachino, the southern tip of Sicily, the lads from our platoon ran forward to create covering fire for us clowns with the Bangalore torpedos. It was then that we came across a wonderful sight! The shells from the heavy warships had completely blasted the barbed wire and machine gun emplacements to pieces. We were ordered to advance quickly to find the coastal road that had figured so prominently on our maps. Looking back, we could see the large L.C.I.'s carrying the Canadians coming in pretty fast. Any thoughts of getting rid of our horrible lumps of exploding metal were soon dashed when we were told that there could be gun emplacements on the road.

The 'road' turned out to be no more than a very broad track and as part of A Troop joined us just in front, it became very congested. Suddenly, the completely unexpected happened. A small group of Italian soldiers burst in on us from the side of the

Landing at Pachino in Southern Italy from an Infantry landing craft

road and immediately screamed, "Surrender"! If it had been left to us, it would soon have been sorted out. But one of the many tragedies of close combat happened. Unknown to us, a group of mixed units had landed far to the left of us and consequently hit the road ahead of us. While it was still dark, we heard fire straight down the road from this group, which sadly killed Sergeant Major Cornish and "Killer" Kilbride, a lance corporal in our section. We were incensed with anger but had to remind ourselves that such 'friendly fire' tragedies were bound to happen. An absurd situation developed when one of our sections, in the dark, came across some land mines and warned the lads behind them. They took their lives in their hands by lifting the mines out of the sand, cutting them up into slices and handing them round - they were watermelons.

As the sun came up, it quickly became very hot and coupled with the presence of very fine sand - almost like flour – and having been on the march, we were soon suffering from thirst. The gun emplacements turned out to be machine gun posts, their crews sitting with daft smiles on their faces and mouthing the magic word "Surrender". It became quite usual to go to the toilet (you made your own) and come back with at least a dozen Italians. (No privacy!) Eventually water wagons appeared and we became more focussed once we had slaked our thirst, as suffering from lack of water started to interfere with our thinking.

We came across a collection of small buildings which turned out to be the homes of the people who tended the olive trees and vines. It was our first experience of the 'padrone' and the peasants who lived on his land and who were completely subservient to him. The distress of these civilians was obvious and we soon found out why. One of the retreating troops, whether Italian or German I don't know, had thrown a dead dog into the well situated in the middle of their homes, and they were suffering from lack of water. As the water wagons were not far away, we had one brought up to the centre of the square and soon the people's thirst was quenched and every utensil that could hold water filled. Later we were informed that a unit of Royal Engineers had extricated the body of the dog, successfully pumped the infected water out of the well, and made the returning water safe.

Because of such acts as this, the people were most welcoming and felt safe in our presence. Treatment of their beasts of burden did rather horrify us, but we were soon told that it was not our business to interfere. We also found out that to call a Sicilian an Italian was to abruptly end a conversation.

After some days of idleness among the olive groves we prepared to advance towards the north of the island. L.C.I.'s appeared and, on boarding, we learned we were making for Syracuse. We landed just south of the town as we were told the harbour was full of craft and, sadly, drowned bodies (another story).

We ended up in a field next to a vineyard and as curiosity got the better of us, we set about exploring the buildings housing huge wine vats. As there was quite a fair amount of wine in them, we retrieved our mugs to sample the red nectar. If the truth was known, it tasted horrible but as it was alcoholic, that part was forgiven.

Daft things became an everyday occurrence. One was caused by Charlie Betts! He decided to explore the other vats on his own but on reaching down with his mug, he lost his balance and fell in! When he climbed out and stood in front of us, we saw that although he wore a Green Beret, the rest of him was deep purple. Pops Manners made him pay thirty shillings for a completely new rig. It took quite some time for his hair to lose the purple hue.

The Commando ship *Princess Emma* appeared just outside the harbour and it was common knowledge that we were to be ready for another landing up towards Messina. However, because the German resistance had all but ended, this move did not take place. This was just as well as I found that my left leg had become very hot and painful, having been caught on the barbed wire on the beach, causing several small cuts. I reported to Dai Morgan, our platoon officer, who commandeered a jeep to take me to the nearest clearing hospital. This was a very large building with a huge red cross plastered right across it. All the passages inside were full of stretchers with the wounded. A naval medic had a look at my leg, pronounced it poisoned and took me to a room with a massive sized bed. He told me to undress and get on the left side of the bed. He said he would be back as soon as possible to lance the infected areas. I was left wondering why I was occupying such a large bed with so many seriously wounded crowding the corridors. I soon found the reason when a paratrooper was brought in with a bullet wound to his right leg. When the medics left, we thought it best to introduce ourselves as we were sharing the same bed. Later two medics appeared, tended to us and on leaving said, "Now that your legs are cleaned up, you will be having a new tenant". We soon knew what they meant when Sid Pritchard from A Troop arrived with a medic who explained that Sid was suffering from concussion. He crawled in from the bottom of the bed and promptly fell asleep.

All the lads of my platoon at Augusta, where I rejoined them after my left knee had been treated in hospital. I am seated on the right – damaged knee still bandaged.

Talking to the para, he told me the sad story about the bodies floating in the harbour. A whole planeload of his battalion had been ordered to jump too early and the majority went into the sea and, weighed down by their equipment, didn't stand a chance.

As Sid Pritchard gradually came to, he became a complete pain in the backside as, whatever the cause of his concussion, it seemed to have dislodged the washer in his plumbing system. It seemed that every half hour he crawled down to the bottom of the bed and disappeared for a leak.

The German bombers arrived as soon as it got dark and we had to stretch the sheet over our heads to defend ourselves from falling plaster. In the morning, we had a magnificent breakfast of fried potatoes and tomatoes, washed down with the same mysterious liquid we had aboard the *Derbyshire*. I thought of causing a riot by asking for a second cup. The medics came round and passed me and the para fit to walk, and by waving a pencil to and fro in front of Sid's face, declared him fit to rejoin his unit, although to me his eyes were still back in last week. We decided to get back to '40' as soon as we could.

It was then that Sid told me the terrible news about the *Princess Emma*. A bomb had exploded beside the ship causing many casualties with many killed. It happened as '40' were going aboard and as the unit was suddenly under strength, the new landing south of Messina was cancelled. We left the hospital considerably saddened.

Two Military Police (Red Caps) took pity on us and took us to their outpost. To our great joy, they gave us a fried egg sandwich and a real mug of tea. Meanwhile, their signaller managed to find out that '40' was now encamped just outside Augusta north of Syracuse and, better still, as soon as transport was going that way, they arranged for us to go with them.

10 Collapse of opposition and over to Italy

WE ARRIVED back with '40' just in time for the evening meal that was McConachie's Irish Stew, a dish that was to haunt us three times a week for nearly two years. As there were always reinforcements to replace our casualties, Buzz Smith made a declaration that if any poor sod presented himself to us with the name McConachie, he would be shot! Peek Frean, the biscuit manufacturer, was another name which was on par with McConachie. Their biscuits were supposed to be nutritious but their taste was akin to the cheapest dog biscuit. In an effort to make them more palatable, we mixed them with goat's milk and crushed grapes, put the unholy mess back into a large biscuit tin, rammed the lid back on and put it on a fire. The idiotic idea was that the finished article would resemble a cake! We soon found out that one does not put an enclosed tin on top of a very hot fire! There was an almighty bang, the sides of the tin burst, the lid was last seen hurtling skywards, and everybody around a twenty yard radius was splattered by a brownish gunge, intermixed with hot ash. Captain Maude observed that a more stringent intelligence test should have been applied to a certain number of us.

We moved towards a small town called Lentini and my section ended up in an olive grove with a large number of fig trees whose fruit, exuded a sweet syrup and were very soft. Obviously the trees should have been harvested. We used the syrup to sweeten the lousy concoction of tea and milk powder supplied in the compo rations. Our little group decided that the only way to make life easier was to descend into nefarious ways to supplement our rations and clothing if necessary. Suffice to say we did very well in all departments, though in some dubious form of redemption, the lads in the Commando never suffered any loss.

We were not the only ones on the scrounge. I often wondered if Pops Manners' words to us, "Be resourceful" ever made him wish he had kept quiet!

One morning, I was ingratiating myself with a friendly family with a tin of corned beef in exchange for a bottle of wine, as the locals seemed to drink a better class than we were ever offered at the drinking dens. While I was there, the signora offered me a hot drink that smelt almost like coffee, which was non-existent. She said it was acorns ground into a rough dust and then roasted over a fire. The result was an acceptable substitute for coffee.

The German opposition north of Messina soon collapsed and we were moved very quickly to the coast to prepare for the invasion of Italy. We were distributed amongst the properties nearest the beach. The L.C.I.'s were already there. This may sound unbelievable but the house we had been allocated seemed very British, with typical furniture. When I opened a drawer I found a bottle of Black & White Scotch whisky and a bag of half crowns. I still wonder to this day who were the previous occupants. Suffice to say, the whisky went the way of all whiskies!

On 7th September the wind got up, followed by torrential rain and we wondered if the landings would be put off. Around 2 o'clock in the morning of the 8th, it suddenly stopped raining and the wind dropped. We were ordered to board quickly as the plan was to land at a small fishing port called San Venere on the west coast of the toe of Italy. The area was called Vibo Valentia (the name on our memorials). The weak resistance of Italian troops was soon dealt with but when two 88s, which was about the best artillery the Germans had (they were situated up on the hills dominating the harbour and the surrounds), opened up on us it was a different situation. The bridgehead was made wider as the Malta Brigade, comprising of Devons, Dorsets and Hampshire regiments, was coming in and was fired on by the 88mms guns. A and B troops were sent to the hills to deal with them. X troop occupied slightly higher ground and was able to witness astonishing acts of bravery by the crews and drivers of transport coming in on huge Liberty ships. As they grounded on the beach, the front doors opened and the drivers, although under heavy fire, drove the lorries full of ammunition and explosives under cover amongst the sheds and then ran back to their ships and continued to drive the remaining lorries off. One of the ships was set on fire but they still carried on unloading. We later learned that they belonged to the Pioneer Corps, a regiment comprised of older men of mixed nationalities. From that day, we held them in the highest regard.

It was during the waiting period before our skirmish at Pizzo railway station when, casting our eyes around the immediate vicinity, our attention was drawn towards a long line of sheds about a hundred yards from us, just above the small harbour. Brad, the youngest lad in our section, and myself were given permission to inspect the sheds to see what treasures they contained. We hammered and tried every door and shutter to gain entrance, but with no success, and so we wandered back to our platoon. It was after fighting had ceased, we learned that a group of the Devon's had entered the vicinity of the sheds and about 60 Germans suddenly appeared with their hands in the air! I thought to myself, 'why the hell didn't they surrender to Brad and me? We might have got a medal! (Wishful thinking).

Dai Morgan and our platoon, comprising 20 men, were ordered to patrol towards the town railway station of Pizzo and, if possible, to take it. Dai decided to keep to the railway lines and on entering the railway tunnel found it full of women and children. As we passed through them trying to see where we were going, some of the women hugged us, which I didn't mind one bit. The only thing I really got pissed off with was being called a brave *English* soldier!

The heat hit us like a sledgehammer as we left the tunnel. Both sides of the rail track were very thick with vegetation, so we split in two and made our way towards the station on either side of the track. There was a bend which shielded us as we came onto the rail trucks. Just before we came in sight of the station, Dai Morgan ordered my section to advance along the other side of the trucks and, with the rest of the platoon, to attack the station. In turn, we were to give covering fire if necessary, but as soon as we showed ourselves, we realised that we had stirred up a hornet's nest. Morgan and the two sections made for the station platform and the rooms around it. They had to duck and dive as there was heavy submachine gun fire coming from that direction, but we managed to get to the first line of buildings. There was a heavy Spandau machine gun set up by the edge of the platform. However, it was exposed to my section coming in from the trucks and was soon disposed of.

It became a bit of a close quarter fight and as this was our first real hand to hand scrap, the discipline ground into us paid off. Dai's lads remained taking on the Germans inside the buildings and we cleared up the ones around the outbuilding. Suddenly Dai gave a shout, pointed up the line and shoved his arms behind his back, meaning, "Get the hell out of it". An armoured truck on rails was bearing down on us. Behind it there seemed to be a regiment of troops. We quickly joined the rest of the lads, crashing through the undergrowth, down a steep embankment and legged it up the beach towards the tunnel when we came upon a strange sight. An L.C.A. was beached just before the tunnel and a solitary sailor had lit a fire and had a bucket on top, full of nearly boiling water. He said, "Just going to make cocoa, want some?" While waiting for a drink, we looked at our casualty list. I was wounded slightly on the hand and leg. Scouse had a bullet in his hand and Brad had a bullet wound in the leg, which luckily had passed through. Sadly Pete Jaggard was killed on the platform. As we were taking sips from the few mugs available, our sailor made a very astute observation, "Been in the wars, haven't you all?"

Our own casualty station was very busy. We found an Army station not far away and the medics were great. We were patched up in no time, reported to Neil Maude, our troop commander, then found a shady spot and relaxed. It wasn't quite true to say that our own casualty station was busy. Our naval doctor was not a very compassionate man and many of the lads were given the distinct impression that they were just a nuisance if they presented themselves to be treated. I believe it was after Termoli that he disappeared with the naval medics. An army doctor and medics took their place and it was the best thing that ever happened. He was Dr Delap, a Belgian, a very fine doctor. He was kind and always found time for you, if a chat was needed or any problem required a sympathetic ear. When we were in action, he would be found where there were the most casualties. It was later at Sarande that he was wounded tending the lads, with the help of the medics.

Throughout the roughly two and a half years of fighting, after every specific battle, a veil was drawn over the action and it was rarely spoken about ever again. It may have been a mental defence to stop one grieving over friends who had died, for it was remarkable how cheerful we soon became. Though while resting at Scalea, twiddling our thumbs, Buzz Smith told me of an instance, though not terrible, which involved himself. While crawling under a railway truck during the fighting at Pizzo railway station, he had wisely applied the safety catch to his Tommy gun. At the precise moment of reaching the other side of the truck, a door suddenly opened at the end of the platform and an Italian soldier appeared, unbuttoned and then relieved himself. Buzz quickly took aim and pressed the trigger, but nothing happened as the safety catch was still on. The Italian by then had disappeared. The next day, Italy capitulated and we both wondered about the soldier and whether he had survived the last day. If he had, he was a lucky man, and hopefully lived to a good old age. He might even still be alive. Or he might have been killed in action!

With our information, the C.O. ordered Y and P troops to take the station with the Hampshires' coming up at the rear. By night time, this was accomplished and everything became very quiet. We dug in and thankfully fell asleep. Early in the morning, the Commando entered Pizzo in force and found the Germans had disappeared. The Army took over and we left for a bit of rest at a small place called Scalea. During our stay there, it happened to be Dai Morgan's birthday. We bought a few flagons of gut rot vino and Dai did well with two bottles of Italian brandy. It turned out to be a great day for him as he was informed that he had been awarded the Military Cross. He had earned it.

On 8th September 1943, the Italians sued for peace. For them the war was over.

The capture of Termoli was an important success. General Montgomery himself came to congratulate 40 RM Commando. Lt Col 'Pops' Manners, Capt Maude, General Dempsey and Lt Dai Morgan are seen with the General in front of the assembled troops.

11 The fight for Termoli

WE LEFT on 22nd September on L.C.I.s for a long trip around the toe of Italy into the Adriatic, calling at Taranto and Bari for clean ups, and eventually camping out at Molfetta. We were told that our next operation was to sail behind the German lines and land in Termoli, which was the H.Q. of the German paratroopers. It was also a very important railway terminal, serving the Adriatic coast as well as the line over the mountains to the Mediterranean. We were to land under cover of darkness, take the town and hold it for three days till the Eighth Army broke through. It was to be our biggest test.

I believe it was 1st October when we boarded our allotted L.C.I.s and made for Manfredonia, just below the actual front line which was the Biforno river, and from there we were to make speed to the landing area just above Termoli.

Being psyched up and very young, we made terrible passengers. As boredom set in on this two day voyage, we decided to have a beauty contest to see who was the most handsome lad in the troop. There were twenty of us picked to mince our way up and down the deck. The rest were just dead ugly. I wished I had had a camera to record for posterity the expressions on the faces of the navy crew. I came in a creditable 4th (I still think it was a fix!)

We arrived at Manfredonia on 2nd October and used the limited time to have a decent wash and our usual Irish stew. The rest of the time was spent testing weapons and filling magazines. I had been elevated to be a Bren gunner. This weapon weighed 28lbs and, together with a heavy Colt pistol and magazines, I carried about 70 lbs in weight.

It was just before midnight, that the L.C.A.s, towed by the

larger L.C.I.s made a dash for the beaches about a mile north of Termoli. As we neared the shore, the L.C.A.s were much smaller and lighter, and hit the beaches with no difficulty but, as we charged on line abreast, we came to a shuddering halt when we hit a sandbank about 50 yards from dry land. Without hesitation, the ramps on either side of the L.C.I. came crashing down onto the water and as quickly as we could, we slid down them and were immersed immediately up to our chests. Holding our guns above our heads, we slowly waded ashore and, judging by the air bubbles at the front and near to me, I surmised that the shorter lads were still with us.

Once ashore, A, P, Q and Y troops made for the harbour, the railway station and the approaches to the town. My troop X, and B were to pass through them and once we were on the road towards the crossroads, we were to go like hell and when we got there, to dig in. Our job was to stop all troops and vehicles coming into the town. My platoon was given the task of taking on everything coming up the road, the rest of the troop scouring the countryside between us and the town, effectively watching our backs. One of the sections between ourselves and the town was led by Fred Usher. His section confronted a German machine gun post. Led by Fred, they successfully attacked the position, silencing it and taking prisoners. Fred was awarded the Military Medal for this action.

The only calamity was that as the wireless sets were waterlogged, we had to revert to the old-fashioned runner system, with lads from H.Q. running between troops relaying all information relevant to each one. When it became light we saw that the road we were covering was very straight for about a mile, giving us plenty of time to get prepared.

We suddenly woke up to the fact that the heaviest weapon we had was the Bren and one anti-tank gun called the Piat. This was extremely cumbersome and to load it, you had to hold the top bars with your hands, your feet on the bottom bars and to pull like hell till a click was heard, then the bomb placed in a funnel at the front. It was imperative that a man was immediately behind the unfortunate who was to press the trigger, as the recoil was so strong. The man behind had to hold the feet of the man firing it, or else he would be thrown backwards. As if that was not enough, there was a small pin attached to the bomb that, in theory, should travel in the same direction as the bomb, but at times it decided to fly backwards, attacking the men behind, consequently the wearing of a steel helmet became compulsory! It was a most hated weapon and caused deep gloom amongst the section to whom it was awarded. A statement made by one lad was, "I would rather leave the f...ing thing behind and attack the tank with my teeth!"

It wasn't long before our first victim, a large military lorry, came trundling up the road. As it got near, I gave a short burst, shattering the windscreen and by the expression on the driver's face, he had obviously dirtied his pants! We had been ordered not to immobilise the lorry or harm the driver so that all vehicles could be driven round the corner by a steep embankment hidden by all transport on the road. We were lucky that the vehicles were just a mixture of lorries, staff cars and the like. There were three occasions when Jerry tried to engage us but they were soon dealt with. Once it was a young German who swung a machine gun towards me and, refusing to surrender, I shot him and as he was wearing a black uniform, not unlike tank corps, we took his pay book and found that he was Hitler Youth. He was only 15.

About mid-day the Germans had obviously got the message that Termoli was not a place to be visited. By the middle of the afternoon, it was very quiet in our sector so I asked Dai Morgan it I could make my way down a deep ditch towards a farmhouse just on the bend of the road and ask if there were any eggs for sale. I knocked at the door and a young boy presented himself. I told him not to be afraid and asked about some eggs, offering to pay. He disappeared and, shortly after, his mother came with a dozen eggs and gave them to me, saying, "Good Fortune" and shut the door. As I was making my way back, I realised the boy was following me. I used all the Italian swear words I could think of to tell him to go back. We lit a fire and by using a steel helmet with the innards torn our, we fried the lot. Amongst the lot of us we only had one spoon. God knows how many times that spoon went round. We didn't bother about foot and mouth! We dug in for the night. With our main wireless sets still out of action, 'listeners' were sent down the road, no more than 200 yards, so they could high tail back to our positions if any Jerry movements were heard or seen. Patrols continually criss-crossed between B and X Troops, as in a small unit. This method effectively closed any space between us and consequently gave our enemy the false impression of facing a much larger unit. Sleep was on a strict rota basis so, of the three platoons in the troop, two were always on full alert, the other at least semi-conscious. Part of our training in Scotland was sleep deprivation and, at the end of that exercise, not only were our reflexes sluggish, but some of the lads became completely hyperactive. Both behaviours could be catastrophic in operations against the enemy and, consequently as a result of the rota system, any situation would be controlled with most of the lads fully alert.

In 1990 40 RM Commando paid a courtesy visit to Termoli. Paddy Humphries and I were guests representing the troops who fought there in 1943. The mayor presented Lt. Col. Wray a Town Crest. The man with the stick was the boy who had sold me eggs. Our interpreter told us that he remembered me.

There was still a fair bit of activity in the town and we relied solely on Peter Fisher, of our intelligence section, to keep us abreast of the situation around us. We asked that if food would be coming up in the morning, could forks be provided? Just after light, a large box of tins arrived which contained a mixture of scrambled eggs, made with egg powder mixed with pieces of bacon, and all we had to do was heat it up. When a person is very hungry, there are no such things as taste buds!

Mid-morning we were notified that the 6/8 Argyll and Sutherlands were on their way, having been landed by sea the previous night to relieve us. We were very tired and looked forward to a hot meal and some sleep. We watched them come up the road. We were dressed in summer gear with a camouflage jacket made specifically to carry ammunition and usually wore our Green Beret, or cap comforter, which was a type of woollen scarf which could be worn on your head, but we carried no encumbrances. They wore steel helmets, a large bumpy greatcoat and had a large pack, small pack, ammunition pouches, and carried a rifle. We wondered what they would manage to do if they were attacked and had to move swiftly to other positions. On talking to them, we realised that they had been subject to an utterly stupid order that whenever a regiment needed reinforcements at a transit camp, men were sent, regardless of which regiment they belonged to, creating a hybrid regiment with very little pride or allegiance to their present unit. I did not find one Scotsman in the Argyll and Sutherlands to talk to and their apathy was overwhelming.

On reflection, regarding the thoughtless reinforcement of battalions within the regiments in the Eighth Army and the untold damage to morale, was it peculiar to the Italian Campaign? We had long realised that we came a poor second to the massive build up towards the invasion of Europe through France. Obviously, at that time Italy did not belong to Europe and it sounded much more dramatic to ignore the simple fact that it did. The very fine Guards Regiments were never affected in that way and one can certainly assume that the High Command drew back from a confrontation with them. As Royal Marines belonged to the navy, we were free from such stupid interference.

To paint a further validation picture of what pride means to a soldier, one must point to the weak resistance put up by the Argylls at the crossroads at Termoli compared with Captain 'Gipsy' Marshall's troop of just over 50 marines. Confronted by over twice their number, instead of defending, they charged headlong into the Germans, completely routing them, killing a third, taking many prisoners and amazingly suffering no casualties themselves.

As it became obvious that 40's role in fighting was confrontational rather than defensive, Pops changed the usual infantry method of attack to a system more suited to ourselves and it more than proved itself at the crossroads. The nine Bren guns remained at the rear, whilst the remainder of the platoon advanced until opposition was met, the Brens then came forward and the fire power was so intense that the Germans kept their heads down. When the Brens stopped, we were on top of them. It earned dividends.

We were found a billet, had some food and lay down on the hard floor and fell fast asleep. The night was very noisy as Jerry was pushing hard to take ground as they most probably realised that '40' were having a rest, and what was against them was subject to pressure. Sure enough, on 5th October, we were ordered to make for our original positions. The bad news was that the so-called Argylls had broken and, if that wasn't enough, the anti-tank battery of guns had been left by their crews! As Royal Marines were gunnery trained, Pops Manners took over the guns and the best part of A Troop became gunners. After a couple of hairy shots, of which we felt the wind, they soon settled down and started to paste the German lines as we advanced in extended order. Buzz Smith made a parting jibe at Jock Morris who was a gunner – "If you blow my head off, I'll kick your arse from here back to Dundee where you come from."

Our own 3" mortars joined in the bombardment of the German positions and as we got into the slit trenches, we found the mortars had done a good job and the Germans didn't put up

Lt. Col. Wray and I guide Paddy Humphries through Termoli. Paddy and Bill Shea were both blinded at Garigliano. They became highly skilled physiotherapists after the war.

much of a fight. However, I lost Joe Nightingale who was killed as we got close, and Ronnie Jacques was wounded but not seriously. The recce regiment followed us up and took over, allowing us to get back into town, and we were immediately sent to the railway yard that had a high embankment overlooking the cemetery, which had been occupied by the Germans for two days.

The Irish Fusiliers were formed up below the embankment ready for the assault on the cemetery. Their attack was certainly hampered by the cumbersome gear they wore and, after putting in a good effort, they were eventually driven back. Pops Manners sensed that when the Fusiliers got back to the railway yard, it would not be long before we would be counter attacked. By bringing all our Brens, plus taking a few from the Fusiliers who gladly gave them up, we ended up with at least 15 guns. Every spare lad was employed filling magazines and to further bolster

Paddy and I lay flowers at the grave of Capt M J Ephraums M.C. who fell at Termoli.

our defences, two Canadian Sherman tanks appeared. By stationing themselves just below the embankment with their main guns over the top, we didn't have long to wait. We were taken by surprise by the strength of the Germans occupying the cemetery as they came at us in waves. However, with the sheer ferocity of our firepower, we were cutting them down before they could get near us. They soon broke ranks and ran. The slaughter was such that we stopped firing maybe sooner than we should have. Casualties in small number from enemy engagements didn't affect you in any great sense but what we had just done, did not seem right. It soon became apparent that the Germans had shot their bolt and had started to retreat northwards. We moved back to our billets in the town, dropped down on the floor and fell asleep. Later, X Troop was ordered to clear the cemetery and stay the night. We decided to sleep in a crypt where the bodies were laid in cavities in the wall, but as the air was so dry, they were mummified. Believe it or not, we all fell asleep! The next day, General Montgomery came to see us and congratulated us all for saving the day. Pops Manners got the D.S.O.

We stayed in Termoli long enough to celebrate my birthday on the 26th. The trouble was that when I remarked my birthday was near, some idiot gave out the wrong day and I ended up paralysed with cheap vino a day early. My actual birthday passed very quietly.

12 Long train trek across Italy

NOW I must digress to write about an occasion, when surrounded by thousands of people, a total stranger and myself were thrown together and by idle conversation found that, because of the war, we had a strong connection with each other.

When the war ended, I became an instructor at Towyn, North Wales, Commando Training Camp. On returning from leave, I arrived at London Paddington Station to travel back to Towyn and, whilst searching for a seat, a lady approached me and asked if I was travelling as far as Shrewsbury. I replied that I was, so she took me to a compartment where a young man sat. Explaining that he was blind and that his sister would be at Shrewsbury to meet him, would I kindly look after him till then? I readily agreed, noticing that he had been badly wounded in the face. We introduced ourselves and started chatting, explaining where I was going and what I was. He asked which Commando did I serve in and when I said '40', he let out a loud exclamation, "Good Lord"! and asked whether I fought at Termoli. When I replied, "Yes", he was silent for a few seconds and then started to describe the railway yard and asked me if I remembered the large wooden shed not far from the embankment. I thought for a moment and replied that that was the H.Q. for the Royal Corp of Signals but was blown apart by a mortar bomb. He replied, "I know because I was a signaller in that shed; most were killed but I was blinded". We realised that we had been only 50 yards away from each other. He was a very brave lad who was getting on with his life and was training to be a telephonist. We duly arrived at Shrewsbury and I handed him over to his sister. We said goodbye and, back on the train, I realised what a small world we live in.

We left Termoli soon after for Molfetta that was to be our main station where, for once, we could settle down and put down roots.

Pops gave orders that we were due a good rest and to continue with light training, to get to know the local people and respect them. When we came into contact with Army units, we should be friendly and at any signs of trouble, to walk away. (His tongue was firmly in his cheek.) Our little section of eight had a nice little billet and the lady downstairs was willing to do our washing. The money must have been a godsend and, as we had never lost our thieving ways, we always had more rations than we could eat, so she benefited from that as well. There was also a Turkish bath style of place where we could indulge in a good soak. The feeling of being clean and tidy was marvellous.

One of the many facets of Pops Manners' ruling of the Commando was to visit every billet at different times and conduct a "Drips" session. The idea was that he would sit down with us and, with no inhibitions, we would give vent to any grievance we had, and if it was relevant to our well being, he did his best to rectify it. Small wonder, when we lost him at Brac, the sense of loss was so deep that it almost became anger.

About that time, when I called at the Quartermaster's to collect the food rations for the next day, I was informed that I was to receive a new form of food called 'dehydrated'. All I had to do was to add water and then cook. I was confronted with four smallish bags and told that they were in order: meat, potatoes, vegetables, and the fourth I took to be some form of pudding. I informed the person at the other side of the counter that there were seven of us, not one! I was told that there was more than enough for seven and ordered to leave. When I got back to the billet and showed our next day's meal to the lads, there were dark mutterings that I had been conned until we found out that the section near to us had been palmed off with the same amount. As we were still solvent, we decided to visit our usual dive but before we left we put the ingredients in our mess tins, poured water on them and then left!

When we made it back to our billet, I decided to look in at our next meal and what a sight! There were three miniature mountains; one looked like mince, another like a mixture of vegetables and the third mashed potatoes. The fourth was still in its inert state. In the morning, we borrowed some pots, boiled the lot and amazingly, it tasted not bad. The white substance, after exhaustive boiling and stirring, still remained in the liquid state. We found out late the next day that it was milk powder!

Christmas arrived and all the billets decided to hold their own party, but we were allowed to gatecrash, as we liked. On Christmas Eve, we went to our favourite drinking place and ended up hardly knowing our way back to our billet. In the afternoon, we had been given extra rations which we gave to our lady downstairs, but we kept a large cylinder of American boneless turkey for Christmas dinner. Ronnie Frost decided to open it and have a slice but as I refused, explaining it was for Christmas Day, he got very stroppy, calling me a Scots bastard. He made for the turkey and, losing my temper, I punched him, forgetting I had a plastic sort of ring with Molly's face on it, causing his nose to bleed. He collapsed on his bed, not from my punch – he was dead drunk. Our little lady came up as usual in the morning with a jug of goats' milk which I used to make porridge (I was the best of a bad bunch at cooking). Ronnie made an appearance looking like a fugitive from the cemetery and asked what the hell did I hit him with? Showing him the ring, I apologised but all he said was, "For Christ sake, take it off the next time".

We had a very quiet day, conserving our energy for the evening. Our spies had informed us that 6 section of Y Troop had gone to the town, spending all they had and had bought a barrel of good quality wine. It was definitely on our list for gate-crashing! Boxing Day too was very quiet, with softly shutting doors, and even the little lady didn't visit us till evening.

We were told the next day we were on the move, but hearing where we were going took a lot of believing. We were to cross Italy by train from the Adriatic to the Mediterranean and with about half of the Eighth Army. We celebrated New Year's Day in a huge cattle truck. It was a helluva long train and the average speed was about 20 miles per hour. We had the marvellous ability to settle down and make ourselves comfortable very quickly and, as usual, got our priorities right. Besides our normal rations, we had managed to thieve two extra boxes plus, if I remember rightly, six flagons of gut rot.

The first day took us into the mountains. The little alpine villages seemed to be completely untouched by the war and the villagers just showed a friendly curiosity towards us. Dawn was breaking when we stopped at a small cluster of buildings to get some water and we were able to wash and shave. There was a chicken farm not far away and, better still, there were chickens that were plucked, gutted and ready for cooking. The original order was that we would be staying for at least two hours, due to blockages on rail transport ahead of us, so we purchased the largest chicken on offer, as there were seven of us. We lit a fire by the wagon, ripped out the soft band of a helmet (we never wore a helmet), stuck it on the fire and threw in the chicken. It had only started to sizzle when we were ordered to board the wagons as the blockage had been cleared. Not knowing what to do with the chicken but determined not to lose it, by using our "Stucka diggers" (a small shovel we attached to our belt for quickly digging in), we gingerly lifted the helmet onto the wagon. Again an order came down the line, "Another twenty minutes". All sorts of suggestions went flying around and we finally settled on the craziest one, namely to dig into the foot thick wooden sleepers which made the floor of the wagon, making chips of wood and place them in the centre of the wagon. The fire which was still burning outside was quickly shovelled in, and the helmet with the chicken balanced on top. The only trouble was that the sleepers were impregnated with some form of oil or grease and soon the wagon filled with smoke. Coupled with the heat of the fire and the stench of burning we spent a good hour with our heads hanging outside for air. Now and again one of us would venture inside to see how the bloody chicken was cooking, or even if it was still there!

A message was passed down the line of wagons enquiring if we were in trouble. We sent a message back that we were just cooking a chicken! We eventually had had enough, doused the fire and let the chicken (which by some miracle looked good enough to eat) cool off. So that some greedy bastard wouldn't pinch the breast, we dismembered it into small pieces and shared it equally. Together with some hard biscuits and a mug of vino, it went down well. (By the way, if somebody said "Hygiene", we surmised he was calling after some female!).

We eventually trundled down through the warm countryside and streamed into the marshalling yards at Naples. It was jam packed with all sizes of wagons, carrying everything from heavy guns to explosives. We were drawn up next to a platform and Dai Morgan came along and told us that Pops Manners had disappeared, swearing he was going to castrate the person responsible for supplying us with food and drink. It could only have been a few minutes before Pops suddenly re-appeared, leading a trail of rather dejected Army cooks carrying urns of tea and separate bags of food consisting of sliced meat, bread and chocolate. The Army lad who approached us remarked that our C.O. must be a right bastard, as he had warned the cook sergeant to get a move on or he would sink his boot right up his arse! We played along with him and pleaded with the lad to get some extra bags as we wouldn't be allowed to eat again till next day. He was soon back with more food and wished us all the best.

Once we had been watered and fed, we turned our attention to the wagons on the other side of us. A young black American sentry came strolling up and we got into conversation with him. He revealed that the trucks were stuffed full of food on route to the American forces. As there were slats on the side to let air in, it didn't take long to get inside. It turned out to be an Aladdin's cave of all sorts of food. There were cases of boned turkey, sides of ham, chocolate, coffee and the inevitable case of beans and corned beef. As everything was tinned, we saw ourselves eating to a very high standard for a very long time. However, as we were busy stacking as much as we could into our wagon, we wondered how the hell we were going to unload it once we had reached our destination. We alerted the lads in the wagons next to us and, passing the news up the line, Aladdin's cave was soon emptied (locusts could have learned quite a bit from us).

I was considered quite a loud mouth, something I could never understand. But being so, I was elected to go to the top wagon and speak to Dai Morgan who, after the usual, "You thieving bastards, etc. etc.", said he would go and see Pops Manners. He was soon back with the message that he didn't want to know, but if we managed to get going before discovery, he expected his share. Dai said that when we got to our destination, we were to make sure there were no Red Caps around. We were to stack the food first and then cover it with our equipment and sit on it ourselves, even if we had to cling to the tailboard.

People might think that in between fighting the foe, we indulged in nothing but thieving and scams. However, it must be realised that we were a very small unit, purely volunteers, and we were there to do the dirty and dangerous work for the Army units to whom we were attached. As to our welfare, they did not want to know, consequently we became quite adept at looking after ourselves (and we liked doing it).

We arrived mid-afternoon at a small town called Vico Equense which was situated within the Bay of Naples and had a small beach. Luckily there was a long convoy of trucks waiting for us and Dai made sure we had the one directly opposite us. We started to pull our equipment out and laid it on the ground, but as the Army driver started to load, we told him the important stuff goes on first. When he saw the food, we had to tell him to stick his eyeballs back in their sockets and if he helped us, he could have some turkey and chocolates. He would, together with his mates on the other trucks, keep his mouth shut.

Our billet was on the coast road and was one of four small apartments. Luckily all the others were occupied by small children. We found out long ago that if you make friends with kids, your feet are under the table in no time, and we found the oldest Mum and within a few days your shirts are washed and ironed for a few liras. Seriously though, I found the Italian people very kind and hospitable. After we had settled in, we shared our ill-gotten gains with the families and, in turn, we could have baths whenever we wanted. One of the young Italian lads, about thirteen, called Guillermo (who we decided to call "Bill") took a shine to us and I reckon he would have moved in with us if we had let him. His thirst for knowledge about Britain and the language was so great that Ronnie Jacques started to teach him English.

Vico Equense was a nice little town situated in the Bay of Naples with Capri in the centre and the lovely holiday resort of Sorrento only a few miles away. We all knew we would soon be "going in again", so Pops Manners didn't bother us and just told us to behave ourselves and that he had notified the Red Caps to lay off! Although it was January, the weather was quite mild. We did not realise that where we were going to was as if it belonged to another planet.

13 To the Garigliano – I am wounded – news of Pops Manners death

IT WAS around the middle of January when we learned that our next mission was to cross the Garigliano river, about 100 miles north of Naples, where British troops were nearly at a standstill. We were under the orders of the 5th Army which was American, although it was a British brigade to which we were attached. Although we were "specialist troops" clothed and armed to be able to move quickly, we were used as ordinary infantry and, as we found out, as cannon fodder. We moved up to the front and on the 17th January into position. As soon was it was dark, our guns opened up and it was reckoned to be about the heaviest bombardment since El Alamein. The noise was mind blowing and communication was by signs or by touching.

By the time we reached the river, the Jerries had started their own bombardment. We clambered into canvas boats and paddled like hell to get across, with orders to dig in and wait till everybody was over. During the crossing, Ron Jacques gave out a yelp and later on he found that his epaulette was gone and he had a burn on his shoulder. It was either a piece of shrapnel or a bullet that had grazed him.

We started to pass through the infantry who seemed to be well dug in, but unnaturally quiet. We started to get opposition soon after, but orders were to keep going and break the enemy line. We were successful for the first three days but, though we were very tired, the infantry seemed reluctant to take over from us. Days seemed to merge but I think it was the fifth day in the evening when we attacked a group of buildings harbouring Germans. During the fighting, I ended up with a dead German crashing down on top of me, re-arranging my face and tearing the muscles of my stomach. Within seconds, my section got me out of it and, taking turns, carried me out through the Fusiliers' lines. The medics took me down to the riverbank and got me across the river in a large flat-bottomed boat with the rest of the wounded. I learned later that it had been a bad day for us in 9 Platoon. Jock Malcolm, Tommy Grey and Happy Day had been killed, Paddy Humphreys and Bill Shea blinded and Frosty had lost his left leg. Freddie Usher had severe wounds to his leg and shoulder and would eventually be going home.

I arrived at a medical staging post where a young Indian doctor cleaned my face and was so gentle cleaning me up, that I was surprised when he told me he had had to dispose of my back teeth as it seemed they were rather loose. I had the good grace to thank him. Soon after, we were shepherded into a fleet of ambulances and, considering we were still practically on the front line, I was surprised to find the ambulance teams were Army nurses. However, they were so calm and efficient it was as though they were in a hospital miles from any danger. As I was more comfortable sitting up, I sat on a pile of blankets, reassuring the nurses that I was all right. I don't know how long it took as there were plenty of stops, some to help the badly wounded and others due to convoy snarl-ups.

We eventually arrived at a large military hospital in Pompeii. All the walking wounded were inducted first, and by the evening everybody was tucked up in bed. After a few days, I felt quite good and back on solids, as long as I ate on my right side. The bruise across my stomach had started to disappear and I began to take an interest in the rest of the lads in the ward. I felt very sad for the ones with limbs missing, with nothing much to do but think. As there were quite a few lads from '40' in the same vast ward, we started to talk about the infantry men we saw lining the road on our first few days after the crossing. They seemed to be completely lost and we were told later that we were lucky to be just physically hurt!

The Queen Alexandra nurses are the most fantastic people. The nurse assigned to me, realising that I was a Scot and that my name was Farmer, asked where I was from. When I said Paisley she suddenly took an interest and asked if I knew an Edward Farmer. I told her that he was my cousin. She told me that he had left the ward two days ago. How they carried on being so calm, faced with such horrendous wounds on the men, yet still found time to talk to you. For instance, the night after I had arrived, I couldn't sleep. My face was very painful and the nurse on duty, noticing I was still awake, felt my face and just walked away. However, she was back soon after with a bowl of ice-cold milk with small pieces of apricot in it. She told me to spoon the mixture into my mouth, retaining is as long as possible. She also came back with a cold compress and laid it on my face. In no time, the pain subsided and I fell asleep. In the morning she was barking out orders as usual and told me that as soon as I was washed and dressed in the hideous pyjamas I had been given, I was on breakfast duty. There was no mention of her kindness, but one knew there was a lot of compassion when needed.

I had been in hospital for about two weeks when I was told I was being transferred to the convalescent camp at Sorrento. I think there were five of '40' beside myself ready to go and it was by sheer chance that when we were in quite a queue signing out, we heard the lad at the desk ask the ones in front if they had any equipment at their base. Some said, "Yes", others who said "No" were directed to the store. I declared my equipment had been lost and was given a full kit bag. The main prize was two New Zealand battledresses which were of a very fine cloth compared with the rough serge of the British counterpart which, at times, 'irritated our very sensitive skin'.

We arrived at the camp in the afternoon, signed in and after a cursory medical, we were given our rooms and told there were no rules but expect to stay off the wine. Sorrento is a beautiful place. Four of us were quite mobile and started to do small runs and walks, as one of the main conditions to get back into '40' was to be perfectly fit. It must seem strange to an outsider that lads were willing to risk their lives just to belong to '40' Commando. The reason is quite simple. Besides the comradeship, the complete trust that we had in each other made us into a united family.

I started to prowl around the place, becoming friendly with some of the Army lads who had been wounded in the same sector as ourselves. However, a tale unfolded of fighting in mountain country, severe cold, shortage of rations and men. When our lads came back, they backed up the Army lads' claims but the saddest sights were men whose minds were so disturbed that their future, and that of their families, was not very good. I said goodbye to four of '40' boys who had been declared unfit for Commando duty due to wounds, and were soon to be going home. I was declared fit after about ten days of easy living and made my way back to Vico Equense. I was amazed by the large number of '40' lads lounging around and it transpired that the Commando had left the Garigliano and was almost immediately sent to the Anzio beachhead.

Pops Manners deliberately refused to order lads like myself back into the firing line, ensuring that the Commando would be so under strength they would have to be relieved.

It was near the end of March when the Commando finally escaped the clutches of the 5th American Army and trundled back over the mountains to Molfetta. We didn't last long in billets and were moved outside the town. We started living in tents, due to persistent "bullying" by the Red Caps. (We had tried very hard to behave ourselves but because of mystery damage to Military Police vehicles and a few bent heads, we were told to get out!)

In early May, we were on the move again and were surprised to learn that we were going to the Dalmatian Islands off the coast of Yugoslavia to bolster Marshal Tito's partisans. We landed on the island of Viz which, though not very large, was the only island in the control of the partisans. We found our main activities were to join M.T.B.s on patrol along the coast and board German supply boats, deal with the crews and then sink the boats. As we were surviving on compo rations and hard tack biscuits, the first time we boarded the M.T.B. in the evening and were served white bread and butter with brisket of beef and a mug of real tea, we thought we were in heaven. The senior officer was Commander Fuller, a screwball if ever there was one! His idea of fun was to cruise between the islands, continuously sounding the Klaxon horn to draw fire from the German garrison to give us a chance of engagement. I wished him great ill health many times.

It was nearly the end of May when we found we had volunteered to go back to Italy (just X Troop) to begin parachute training. (It is amazing how people look after your welfare!) We had barely landed at Brindisi when we were ordered back to Viz. Shortly after we had left Viz, '40' and '43' Commando were ordered to join a Partisan Brigade to attack the largest island in the group called Brac. It was the first time the Marine Commandos had fought closely with the Partisans who, with the wild discipline they displayed, cost us dearly. When the news broke that Pops Manners had died, it was as if a large bunch of young lads had lost their father.

It was on 2nd June that the raid on Brac was carried out and the day that our well beloved Pops died of multiple wounds sustained on two separate occasions. From information obtained from the Germans and conveyed to the Swiss Red Cross, Pops died later the same evening.

A mixed group – commandos and partisans on the island of Vis, Yugoslavia. The wild discipline they displayed cost us dearly

Pops Manners came from Sea Service to become the commanding officer of X Company of 'A' Royal Marine Commando, one of the first companies to be formed from the hundreds of volunteers who, like me, became a member of the first Commando. In the selection process he showed himself very able to size up men who stood before him, sending quite a lot back to their units judged unsuitable after a few shrewd questions. After Dieppe and following the death of Lt. Col. Picton Phillipps he was promoted to C.O. of 40 Royal Marine Commando. His unorthodox ways quickly spread throughout the unit. He devised a way of instant punishment – informing our landladies that we were to be incarcerated for a week after the training had finished for the day. He knew of our respect for our landladies – our surrogate "mums", and that we would not betray them by going out against their wishes.

It was many years after the war when we started to meet on a regular basis and eventually cut ourselves loose from the rather stale reunions organised by the Army Commando. We started to organise our own gatherings and during the reminiscing, Pops Manners' demise always came to the fore. Once, a very pertinent question was raised. "Could his death have been avoided?" One answer contained a large grain of truth. Lt. Col. Churchill of 2 Army Commando always had the bagpipes screeching, even in the heat of battle. The Germans, being no fools, would be well aware that where this wailing sound came from, there would be senior figures present and a concentration of mortars around that area might wreak dividends. Most would be doubtful of such a theory but I am not, and many others have subscribed to that way of thinking.

14 A rest in Malta and then we invade Sarande in Albania. Malaria recurs – then back to Turi

WHEN we realised that because of Pops Manners' death there would be a new commanding officer and the usual retinue of new N.C.O.s, we talked about putting in for a transfer. Being volunteers, this was our prerogative. However, after a long discussion, we realised we would be split up and as we had become inseparable, it was decided to stay and take whatever was coming. We soon learnt our new C.O. was to be Lt. Col. Sarkey and, as we were seriously under strength, a large draft of untried reinforcements joined us. Many were junior N.C.O.s who tried to pull rank on us veterans and caused open warfare. As we had such a high opinion of ourselves, they were a long way down the scale in our estimation.

As our old organisation was turned upside down in this way, the return of 'dead men's kit' was delayed until the rest of the close comrades of the men who were killed went through their kit. The reinforcements objected, thinking that we were defiling our former comrades' possessions, so they were forcibly ejected from the process. The truth of the matter was that although marvellous friends and first rate soldiers, some were married and also had girlfriends and so we went through letters and small items of a personal nature, destroying girlfriends' letters and the like as surely the wife would be suffering enough heartache. Our new Troop Commander, Captain David Angus, a Scot from Stirling, fully understood that in our small and tightly-knit unit it was the right thing to do.

One evening, as we sat in our billet bemoaning the fact that we were skint, I spied this mismatched pair of boots that didn't seem to belong to anyone. One was size four and the other nine and a half. I grabbed them and wended my way towards the house of ill repute. (They handled everything but guns!) Keeping the boots on the move in my hands, I received 200 lire for them. Returning to the billet, I told the lads that night was saved and we were off to the nearest dive to spend it. After a few brandies, we decided that the next morning we would keep a good lookout for an Italian with a slight limp, as he was surely the guy who had bought the boots.

On 17th August we sailed for Malta and a long rest. By now we realised that the old and the new had to knit together in an effort to become the unit that had been. We were lucky with our Troop Commander.

We had a good time in Malta once the air had cleared. Three of us decided one day to spend the evening at Sliema and near the end of our boozing spree, we found that we were broke but would have liked another drink. We entered a small bar and ordered three rums, which we quickly downed. A huge black man appeared at the bar demanding the money. Being a complete idiot, I pointed to my nose and told him to take it out of that, which he promptly did. I disappeared out of the door, landing on my arse. Don and Charlie grabbed me and we disappeared quickly towards the camp.

Next morning I realised what a fool I had been. In spite of our childish antics, we usually all paid our way. I went back in the evening to the bar and saw the black barman. After eyeing each other I apologised and offered to pay. He said, "As a fellow Scotsman, we will shake hands". Keeping a straight face, I asked him where he came from. He said that his mother came from Greenock where she had met his father, a merchant seaman. After his birth, the family settled in Malta before the war. We became good friends and spend many an evening, arguing about football. He was a very likeable man. I still wince when I remember our first meeting.

We left Malta for Monopoli south east of Bari around the middle of September and settled in tents, wondering where next? It seemed that Colonel Sankey was a stereotype commanding officer, who got out of bed in the morning and expected to survey his troops, whereas Pops had let us find our billets and fend for ourselves. Now we were back in tents, with morning parades and communal feeding. It was obvious that '40' was going to be turned back into something resembling a normal military unit. The 'free spirit', was to be suppressed and normal heel clicking and saluting were to be resumed. The fact was that of all the Army and Royal Marines Commando units, '40' was the most experienced and most successful Commando, mainly due to Pops Manners' unorthodox ways of commanding. One of his sayings was, "All men are equal in battle, but by the end of the day make sure you are more equal than the enemy". When it really mattered, our discipline was second to none.

In the last week in September we received news that we were embarking at Bari for an assault on Sarande in Albania. This was a small fishing port, important to the Germans as they could use it for supplies between Greek coastal areas. Corfu was only a couple of miles across from it and it was known that the Germans were gradually getting out of Greece.

We landed on the beach north of Sarande in the early hours of 24th September and were confronted with very steep terrain consisting of rock and gorse, the combination of both making it very hard going. The first few days were dry and not too cold. Patrolling was very active at night as the Germans closed themselves down and only showed themselves during the day. Then the rains came! For eight days it poured relentlessly and as we had no cover except a groundsheet and gas cape each, we suffered. We carried on patrolling but, as the rocks became very slippery and sharp, our boots started to split.

During the eight days of rain, we became very cold and stiff in our bones, but stoicism was second nature to us in hellish conditions. But, as usual, something always came up to raise a smile. We all liked a smoke but even to expose a cigarette for a second, it became a sodden brown mush, just fit to throw away. Then I had an idea. I crawled underneath a cleft of rock, putting my groundsheet on the ground and tucking it over my legs, I pulled my gas cape which was waterproof over my head, positioned my cigarette tin with lid already loosened and my lighter next to it. I loosened my jacket and stuck my hands into my armpits and rubbed like mad to get them warm and dry. I then took a helluva risk with my marital prospects, and lit my cigarette. I was wallowing in my success as I puffed merrily away. But as smoke started to seep our of my gas cape, it was soon noticed and I heard a voice exclaiming that that bloody piece of haggis was smoking. Within minutes, there was a queue of hopefuls with their cigarette tins imploring me to light up for them. Being a generous type, at first I didn't mind, but as time went by my eyes started to stream and my throat became very hoarse. I had to call it a day. I swear I was still breathing out cigarette smoke for hours.

The steep terrain of rock and gorse made for very hard going, made worse by torrential rain. Manhandling mortars and support artillery into position was gruelling work.

Artillery units duly arrived and, taking a chance that German guns guarding the harbour could not traverse around far enough, in the pouring rain we hauled our mortars and base plates, which weighed nearly a cwt. up a steep cliff. We had lads clinging onto the cliff face every two or three yards and by handing the mortars and plates to them, gradually passed them up. We did the same with the Raiding Support Regiment troops' small howitzer guns, which could be stripped down.

Part of H.Q. had been given the task of taking charge of mules to carry supplies. Peter Fisher's mule was so full of fleas that he eventually was alive with them and, in desperation, walked into the sea right over his head and calmly walked out again. As Peter exclaimed, "I couldn't be any wetter anyway".

On 9th October, all the guns we had at our disposal opened up and in the early hours we started to move towards Sarande, knowing that if we succeeded, we would have a roof over our heads. Part of our troop had to join some engineers to clear mines on the beach. My platoon was given the task of clearing the gun positions just in from the beach, and then to head generally towards the town. It was hard going for as soon as we had cleared one hilltop, we had to descend and take the next one.

As we scrambled down the last small valley and started to climb again, we got a considerable shock as out of nowhere, three Germans stood up with their hands in the air. They had two heavy machine guns. We asked the officer why they had not engaged us. He said that when he saw we were British, he ordered the two machine gunners to surrender as they would be treated humanely. Talking to him later, he said that he had fought in Russia and was then sent to Albania. As he had been badly wounded and his family were nearly wiped out during the bombing of Dresden (his home town), he had made up his mind that when the opportunity arose, he would give himself up.

At the crest of the hill, we were ordered to dig in as the rest of the troop coming behind us had come under sniper fire from a row of buildings to our left. Buzz Smith, another Bren gunner, and me crept as near as we could and during our covering fire, the lads were able to join us. As we ran down the hill, the rest of the Commando came in from both sides, but the returning fire from the Germans increased and three of my section were wounded. Luckily no-one was killed.

The town was typical of the country itself, very much like Yugoslavia. The streets were narrow. Street fighting is horrendous and frightening at best, and it was compounded by this narrowness. By the afternoon however, all resistance had ceased and mopping up was carried out very swiftly before nightfall.

The next morning, we found a lot of the buildings were booby trapped, so we grabbed the German engineers who we were certain had set them up, and made them march in front of us and in no time the town was clear. In the evening, I felt bloody awful with shivering and sweats. Our medic, Yorky, soon diagnosed Malaria. The next day I was shipped off with the wounded to hospital in Brindisi.

I had blood type malaria, one of the nurses explained to me. I would have recurrences for many years till it finally left my system. She was right. It was 1960 before the attacks ceased. As I had gone a few days without treatment, I had to drink quinine neat. This was foul giving me mouth ulcers, black teeth and I became quite deaf. In between bouts of shivering and sweating, I was able to get up, help with the tea rounds and visit the lads who had been wounded. I was there for fourteen days and as Brindisi was now hundreds of miles from the fighting, most of the patients were non-combatants. Consequently the nurses treated us like royalty. I visited Dr. Delap in the officers' ward and he was quick to tell the other officers about '40'. While I was in hospital, '40' crossed over to Corfu. The lads were overwhelmed with the response of the people. Jimmy Lennon stated afterwards that they had fought valiantly to keep their virginity but had to give in in the end!

After a couple of weeks, '40' returned to Monopoli for a well earned rest. Then X Troop moved to Turi, south of Bari. I noticed coming back from hospital, that there was an aura of quietness, not the usual noise and friendly insults flying around. The vast majority of the lads, their clothes perpetually wet, had all suffered from a mild form of trench foot, and a rawness around the groin and armpits after the heavy rainfall at Sarande. But as almost immediately, they moved over to Corfu they were able to have treatment, wonderful hot baths, and clean clothes but somehow the 'spark' was missing. Short of funds, and also in a new town, we pooled what Lira we had, bought a couple of flagons of wine from the family across the landing from us. (I think I already mentioned the wine the locals buy is far superior to the gut rot, the taverns palmed off on us). It was after the first flagon had disappeared, the atmosphere gradually changed to the usual ribaldry, and the abuse of the English language, the tongues started to loosen, and it was Don Cass, who suddenly, and rather forcefully spoke: "The weather, the food, and let's face it, our morale was the pit's, how the hell we got off our knees, and took Sarande, I will never know". A few moments of silence followed. Tommy Jebb summed it quite nicely when he remarked "It was a proper bastard, but the few weeks in Corfu, made up for it". It was if a cloud had lifted from us, and by the time the other flagon was finished, we were back to our usual noisy, uncouth deliberations as to what to get up to next.

    We found a decent billet for the seven of us, helped by a very friendly Italian lad who arranged with us and the nuns in the convent to have the use of the baths, provided we supplied more than enough wooden logs for the very antiquated boiler. The women who worked in the convent agreed to wash our kit for an agreed sum. We thought that the children who always seem to be around belonged to the women. However, one night I managed to have a bath before six o'clock, the time the nuns shut the gates for the night. The women had already left but the children were still there and had started to wash and it seemed that they were getting ready for bed. I asked about the children and was told that they were war orphans who the nuns had agreed to look after until the day they would find a home, something I was quite sure would happen. The Italians are extremely family orientated and are very kind to children.

121

15 Christmas is a time for children – even in war

ABOUT a couple of weeks before Christmas, I received a very substantial parcel from my eldest sister. There was amongst other things from the family a large square biscuit tin, inside which was a marvellous fruit cake. To think of the post service today, a parcel like that had survived all the way from Scotland and arrived whole. My first inclination was to devour it but then, collectively, we decided to keep it till Christmas.

About three days before Christmas, four of us were wallowing in a very hot bath (we had a bath each) when Don Cass suddenly shouted, "I have a brilliant idea. Let us invite the kids and if we steal enough compo boxes which contained chocolate and boiled sweets, together with the cake, we will give them a party". We put it to the nuns who, in turn, were over the moon and readily agreed. Putting the cake away, swearing to shoot the first one who even picked a currant from it, we suddenly found a purpose in life. 'A bit of thieving'. We contacted the other sections who agreed to give us their chocolate rations. Thinking of the fruitcake, we thought it was a pity we could not find some icing sugar to cover it. Then, showing how naïve we could be, Buzz Smith and myself decided to pay a visit to the nearby military hospital to scrounge. We presented ourselves at the matron's office. On seeing her, I was on my best behaviour and said, "Good morning Ma'am". She replied that it was obvious that I wanted something for nothing and added that I only had to listen to the quiet to realise that none of our lot was there. I explained about the fruitcake, that we were giving a Christmas party for the orphans and had she any icing sugar. She burst out laughing and explained that icing sugar was certainly not on their list of priorities and that it took a bit of believing that we were doing this for the children. She then became serious and asked us to bring the cake and explained that a mixture of glucose D and gelatine makes a decent substitute. We came back with the cake and she promised it would be ready next morning. Sure enough, when I presented myself, the cake was beautifully iced and the nurses had put small coloured sweets on the top.

Christmas morning was spent cleaning the billet getting ready for the invasion. The family next to us lent chairs and an extra table. The mother and daughter laid everything out very nicely and as she left, she turned round to us and said, "Your mothers should be very proud of you all". Don Cass summed it up very well when he said that it was nice to be human again, even for such a short time.

We trooped up to the convent to collect the children. They looked lovely in their white dresses. On their heads were small flowers arranged by the nuns. We promised we would bring them back by 6 o'clock and by joining hands, we reverted to childhood ourselves, making an almighty racket running down the street towards our billet. Our neighbours, with the help of tins of McConachie's Irish Stew and every vegetable we could find, made a wonderful soup. Together with corned beef sandwiches, they made the first and second course. Then came the 'Cake'. The squeals from the kids were deafening. We had to jump in quick to grab a slice for ourselves.

With Jimmy Lennon's mouth organ, we taught them 'Ring a ring a roses', musical chairs and then with the kids on our backs, we had horse racing up and down the corridors. Six o'clock came very quickly and giving each kid a bag of sweets, a bar of chocolate and 20 lire (worth about 20 pence in today's money), we took them home. The nuns could not thank us enough. We gave them all the left over tins of meat and corned beef. In 1944 in a small Italian town, nuns from a convent happily handed over eight small girls to foreign troops, knowing that they would be safe. How times have changed.

16 Our palace in Corfu – The last battle at Commachio

IT WAS early January when we learnt that we were going back to Corfu. Anarchy had returned to the island, made worse by the incursion of ELAS troops from the mainland. They were dyed-in-the-wool Communists intent on taking over the island. Facing them was just a small garrison of Greek troops withdrawn from Italy so the decision was made that '40' should return to Corfu and sort things out. We were given carte blanche as to how we carried it out. We immediately confronted the ELAS and invited them to leave or to stay and become permanent fixtures – six feet under!

The operations carried out under the command of Lt. Col. Sankey were successful, especially in Corfu, because of his superb handling of the political situation.

Our section was a few miles outside the town of Corfu and, as well as a few small villages, there was a huge building surrounded by orange and lemon groves and vineyards. The locals called it "The Kaiser's Palace", as it belonged to the Greek Royal Family who were of German origin.

Whether one could call it luck or not, our section was given the immediate area around the Palace. It was empty with no-one responsible for it, so we decided to make it our bedding down place. We entered through very large decorated doors with the Greek royal crest carved on both sides and found ourselves in a huge hallway with numerous doors and passageways, opening up on each side. We opened the largest door and found ourselves in a bedroom with a bed that took up half the room. There were large statues at every corner and, without thinking, we opened one of the doors and threw our equipment in and shut the door. We ingratiated ourselves with the locals and had our Mconachies in one of the homes nearby. They were more than delighted that we were staying around the area and felt safe.

It was dark when we got back to our 'billet', staggering around in the dark and eventually found the room with our blankets. In the morning, we discovered the kitchen – you could have held a dance in it. We got the old 'Aga' type oven going, ready for our *'Cordon Bleu'* meals. As it was the Italians who garrisoned the island in the early part of the war, we found it helped us greatly that we could converse quite well with the local people. We were able to make them fully understand precisely what changes in administration of the island would mean to them. There were a few skirmishes but after that there were casualties on the ELAS side only. They eventually departed.

Food was brought in by United Nations Relief and Rehabilitation Administration. Inflation was soon dealt with by the introduction of the Greek drachma at a controlled rate, so civilians were able to go back to work and to be paid. The police force was put under notice to shape up or get out. A small Greek government was formed and, together with the friendly Greek troops under General Zervas, the island slowly returned to normality.

The former summer palace of Mon Repos called by the locals 'The Kaiser's palace' because of the German origins of the Greek royal family. A marvellous billet.

We returned to Italy in mid February to Turi and were immediately put under notice to move at any time. In the middle of March, we moved north to the river Reno, relieving No. 2 Army Commando who we rated very high. Till the end of March, we occupied dugouts by the river edge and carried out incessant patrolling. The countryside was in stark contrast to Albania. It was flat and swampy, cut into many pieces by small streams and dykes.

Fate plays many tricks on people. Lofty Bradley and me, as we had completed the same amount of patrols, tossed as to who was going on the next one. Bradley lost, went on patrol, stepped on a mine and lost both his legs. (He was a tough chap. In spite of his loss, he built his own bungalow after the war.)

It was very wet underfoot and the damp air made our stay so uncomfortable, that the intelligence staff gave the order we receive a tot of rum every evening.

On 1st April, the rest of the Commando, together with the infantry, made an attack on the large piece of high ground immediately in front of us. The rest of the Commando brigade attacked from the sea. X Troop's job was to pretend that we were going to cross the river. We hauled boats with dummies inside to the river's edge, starting up heavy enemy machine gun fire. We

Lofty Bradley (on the right) and me. We tossed a coin to see who went on the next patrol. He lost, hit a mine and lost both his legs.

drew their gunfire and mortars on to us. We just dug in, holding our fingers to our ears. By morning, it was all over and by the scenes of devastation and the plight of the Germans, and the dejection of the prisoners, we had a strong feeling that it was near the end of the war. We had a few days' respite and we were then told we would soon be making the lunge towards the Menate bridge and the pumping station at Commachio.

As we moved towards dry ground and our last objectives, we were confronted by terrible sights of dead horses still tethered to guns and lorries. The smell was appalling and the complete disorder was further indication that the end of the war was near. The only road near our area was full of locals making their way to our rear, correctly surmising that the important bridges and pumping station were our objectives. At the beginning of the war, seeing the newspaper or newsreel pictures of long processions of people deprived of their homes during the German advance through Belgium and France, one had viewed it all with a certain detachment. But this was a completely different situation, this was real and I was part of it. I felt a great compassion for those innocent people; they showed no animosity towards us.

There was an ominous silence from Jerry's guns as though they were waiting for us with all that they had left. The Germans from our hard-won experience were on the whole very good and proud soldiers. Now the end was near we knew we were probably still in for a helluva fight.

On 10th April, the entire Commando Brigade moved up towards Lake Commachio. '40' once again seemed to have the most important objectives. Firstly to capture the pumping station, then to remove explosives and get to the Menate bridge so that the Queen's Regiment, who would be following us in Fantails, (tracked vehicles that could move in mud and very wet ground,) could consolidate the position.

The night after we arrived, a load of beer arrived and throwing caution to the wind, we lit a fire and gathered round it. Captain Belbin, our Troop commander, appeared with two bottles of whisky, which gave each of us a good tot.

We spent the next day in final preparation for the attack, reading and remembering every word of our orders as we all realised this battle was going to be one of the most difficult we had ever faced. The contour map showed that once we had crossed the Menate, which was quite narrow, there was going to be an endless crossing of streams and muddy banks, until we got within 300 yards of the pumping station. With the Germans in control on the left flank, X Troop had to cross a dyke adjacent to the lake and get behind their lines. We rid ourselves of anything that might rattle, stuffing paper between magazines. We used burnt wood to blacken our faces. We became pensive and quiet. I knew the lads were all thinking the same as myself. We had fought at each other's side for nearly three years and were quite certain that this battle could be our last. Would we survive or fall at the last hurdle?

We started off just after 2 o'clock in a long file, slowly making our way along the dyke. We had two R.E. lads slightly in front with mine detectors. At times we had to halt to make sure everybody was still in close contact as there was complete silence, and just by touching the one behind, we carried on. Eventually we reached the river. Captain Belbin tied our ropes together and tying this long lead rope to his waist, half waded and half swam to the other side. Anchoring himself to the ground, we were able to pull ourselves across. The cloying mud made progress very slow and as dawn was slowly coming up, we dreaded that a German voice would challenge us. Luck was with us and the entire Troop, ten of us, lined up on the bank. But as soon as we started to advance, the Germans were alerted and we were immediately under machine gun and mortar fire. The ground we were crossing was stinking mud. It didn't seem to matter whether we were on high or low ground. As we got near the pumping station, there in front of us was perfectly flat ground. Ideal killing ground in the Germans' favour.

P and Q Troops were being heavily shelled by self-propelled guns. The C.O. ordered an air strike. Soon after, four Hurricanes came screaming over, turned, and as they came back again, released their bombs and the killing ground erupted. We went forward on the run and the bomb craters were our salvation. Things were a bit sticky fighting in the pump station but by early morning it was all over. By some miracle, I found that the old reprobates were still standing.

I made my way over to Q Troop to see Ronnie Foster who had been promoted and consequently had to leave us. When I enquired, I was told Ronnie was dead. In all the years of fighting, one's feelings were controlled, but this time I cried my heart out. There were many sad occasions during the war when friends died or were so badly wounded that they went home to recuperate. We were no strangers to tragedy. In this last battle at Commachio, there were two extremely poignant occasions involving a corporal and two marines who had never been in combat. As things were, they should have been given duties away from front line activities. The young corporal joined us at the river Reno a few days before we made the crossing. Most of us had been out on patrol every other night. The corporal went out on the third night of his arrival but did not come back. In a scuffle with Jerry, he was shot. A week later, a letter came for him and as it is a duty to read it before

The pumping station at Menate.

his death was made known to his family, the contents hit us very hard. He had just become a father.

The two marines arrived at our platoon to join us. When we found out that they had just finished training in England and had been sent straight out to us, they were made extremely unwelcome. After nearly three years, all the sections within the platoon had become so battle hardened; there was no room for inexperienced men. Within my section, seven of us knew each other's thoughts, habits and, above all, had complete trust in each other. We felt safe within our own little group. There was no room for strangers. The two lads were told to stay to the rear of the section, to keep their safety catches on and do nothing till ordered. The fighting soon commenced and at the finish, the oldies were still standing but the two lads were dead! I did not even know their first names. We knew that it was a stupid act to commit those lads so soon.

The Queen's Regiment came through our lines and we retreated to a small village nearby. We were caked in mud but all we wanted was water and to collapse on a dry piece of ground. By the evening, I was feeling rough and had started the shakes and sweating. It was malaria again. I was taken to a small hospital near Ravenna and remained there for ten days.

A few days after that, the war ended.

17 Serving brandy to the enemy – On the loose in Rome

ALTHOUGH the Commando hadn't moved very far I found the disbanding of the unit had already started. All senior officers had gone and an unfamiliar captain was in charge. He told me to report next morning to take charge of a work detail, but when I caught up with the lads I was told not to take any notice. Everybody had been told the same at some time or other. The drill was just to disappear, do a bit of scrounging and make life as comfortable as possible.

We had been through hell and back at times, now we were dispensable and as we were volunteers, we did not belong to any regiment or battalion. We were a nuisance and the authorities seemed at odds as what to do with us.

In the middle of May, we were on our way to become prison guards, guarding S.S. prisoners. We thought we may be having trouble with them but they seemed quite passive till one night, not long after we arrived, an officer approached us and told us rather an unlikely story, which proved to be true. The day the war ended, a large group of them broke into a bank and they had in their possession over a million lira. However, it would be no use for us to storm the tents as we would never find it but he had an idea that might interest us, seeing what we were. (I don't know what he meant by that remark!) They would give us enough money to buy bottles of brandy, which we would keep on our side of the wire. After dark, they would line up on their side, receive two glasses of brandy and pay ten times the value. They promised that they would never demand more than two glasses. From then on, there was the spectacle of three tables with booze on it, opening the bar dead on 1 o'clock in the morning – six of us doling it out and three taking the money! We made a fortune. It only lasted about ten days when we were relieved by an Army unit. The Germans accepted that they would have nothing to do with such shenanigans and we found ourselves wishing each other good luck.

The good news was we were going on nine days' leave to Rome. We arrived at a transit camp with what seemed like hundreds of servicemen on leave. The one meal we had was horrendous and the fact that we were supposed to sleep there every night made us more certain that we wouldn't be.

The second day we went into Rome and did some sightseeing. In a drinking den not far from the Coliseum, we met some New Zealand tank crews and ended up sleeping in their billet just outside Rome. On the third day, once we had sobered up, we hired a horse carriage and saw the sights in comfort. The Red Caps' faces were a study, because those contraptions cost an arm and a leg. They didn't realise that that was precisely what we had. In the afternoon when we were having a quiet drink in a classy restaurant, a group of R.A.F. pilots came in. They seemed quite interested in us and eventually invited us over to their table. One of them uttered one word, "Commachio". We asked how they knew. It turned out that theirs was the squadron that had saved us from a nasty turn of events by the pumping station. They took us back to their mess and all I can say is that two days of my life went by and I was not very conscious of them. We were treated like royalty and for the next five days, we had the time of our lives and arrived back at the transit camp skint! Soon after we were told we were going home.

18 Molly meets my family and we decide to marry

WE ARRIVED in Southampton on 26th June. The next few months were spent at Towyn, in North Wales in an atmosphere of intense boredom. Trousers with sharp creases, shiny boots and orders in high cultivated squeaky voices were the order of the day. We moved to Basingstoke from where a detachment of us were bussed up to London to take part in the Victory Parade. At one point we were ordered to remove our Commando flashes. We demanded to see the Admiralty order concerning Commando flashes. But of course, there was not one.

It was the beginning of May 1946 when I was handed a large kitbag and a brown box and joined a queue to receive my civilian clothes *and* a trilby hat, which I never used. The suit was of very poor material and I wore it to work. I managed to get a travel warrant to Paisley with a deviation to Sandown to spend a few days with Molly, as a lot of water had flowed under the bridge since we had spent some time together.

Molly and I had met when the future of the whole world appeared so shaky that we had never dared to make a firm commitment to each other. But the thought of Molly had kept me going all the time we were apart. Now it looked as though our moment had arrived. She had been born and bred on the Isle of Wight in surroundings far removed from the tougher world of a Scots working class community. I asked Molly to come to Scotland to meet my family where in an industrial area with people living cheek by jowl, strangers were regarded with a degree of suspicion. But Molly, being Molly with her open and cheerful nature, soon won everybody over.

My family decided to hold a party. I told my Mum that the dress she was wearing matched her snowy white hair. Taking me to the kitchen window overlooking the front gate, she said: "This is the reason I have snowy white hair. I was drawn to this window every morning for three and a half years, looking for the telegram boy with the bad news for the families around and was nearly physically sick until he passed. But now you and Tommy are safe I am content".

Back on the Island, a friend of Molly's who was employed at a small boatyard situated on the Duver, St. Helen's, enquired if I was interested in a month's work helping to bring across from Chichester harbour a number of decommissioned motor torpedo boats and a small number of assault landing craft, and to beach them in Bembridge harbour. Being at a loose end I accepted. Molly was rather surprised as the one very important topic we tended to skirt around was the eventual place where we would make our home, Scotland or the Isle of Wight! We both agreed this job would give us more time to decide, and, of course, give us more money to put away.

The next few weeks I thoroughly enjoyed - bringing the boats over. I always seemed to be the one at the wheel going into the harbour. The routine was to steer hard to starboard, then hard to port and charge up the embankment. The M.T.B.s were built to run aground so no damage was done and I found the excitement I felt was almost akin to the war years. These boats had become very familiar in the Commando days. The entrepreneur who had bought the craft wanted to make them into houseboats, so there was plenty of work for good craftsmen. He made more money selling the huge Packman engines that he paid for all the craft. The manager sent for me and asked if I was interested in staying as I had told him of the building courses I had undertaken before the war. I had also started to sign-write again, and was determined to become proficient.

The harbour was alive once more as the owners returned. Many, like myself, had served in the Forces, and started to spruce up their craft. I found myself busy painting names and, as I had a very steady hand, the plimsoll lines.

In August we decided, as I had two weeks' holiday, to travel to

Paisley to see my family and officially become engaged. Bessie, my sister, laughed when she told me what Mum said to her: "Don't you think that the world is a strange place at times and what can happen? Just think, our Jimmy marrying an English girl. Who would have thought it?"

After a couple of days, we told the family we were going to Glasgow to buy our engagement rings. Within an hour, Bobby, my eldest brother, had booked a large room at the Halfway House, a pub about three miles outside Paisley. I did not realise the size of my family, which included in-laws, aunts, uncles, nephews and cousins I had barely heard of. An accordion player arrived, and as the night went on, it became noisier and I realised that Molly was sampling everybody's drink, and was becoming rather the worse for wear. The party ended just before eleven o'clock so that we could catch the tramcar home. As we boarded, we had to climb up the stairs as downstairs was full. Molly sank into a seat just at the top of the stairs and, as I passed her, I innocently said to her, "Behave yourself". Before I reached my seat further along, there was a reply from Molly, "Don't tell me to behave myself. You know what you can do with this". We then watched with amazement a small engagement ring come sailing through the air towards me and disappearing in the slats on the floor. We then had the spectacle of the entire top of the tram on their hands and knees (with the exception of Molly) trying to find the ring, and eventually it was found. Dad made an acute observation – that red heads tend to be like that!

The next day everybody carried on as if nothing had happened and a very subdued Molly suddenly said, "Did you find it?" We announced that it was in our possession and then realised that we should stop teasing her as we saw tears, but soon had her laughing and suggested she should take the pledge! I then told Mum and Dad that I had decided Molly and I would be making our life on the Island. They fully understood. Mum said, "The greatest thing that happened to us was that you survived. Molly will be good for you and don't forget us".

As it was still the summer season on the Island, we both took evening work to swell our coffers and again good fortune smiled down on us. I was helping a friend to decorate his house, which he had rented from a Mrs Moorman, an elderly lady who lived nearby. The house was directly opposite the Castle Inn, our second home during the war. Three doors up from the house, 21 Fitzroy Street, the tenant had recently died and left the property in an appalling state. Mrs. Moorman, knowing Molly and I were being married in the near future, offered us the house to rent with a view to buying it. If I put the house in order, I would be paid for the work and pay no rent till we moved in. Giving us roughly two months to make it liveable, we decided that 9th October would be our wedding day and it would be in the Methodist Church in Station Avenue. (It is now a second-hand furniture store).

Though I was quite happy at the boatyard, being more or less my own boss, the fly in the ointment was the general foreman who deeply resented the freedom I had and as I did not like the man, coupled with my built-in arrogance towards people I did not care for, this had to come to a head. It did on a Friday afternoon. The foreman had rigged a bosun's chair onto the mast to fix a halyard to the top of the masthead. As I was varnishing inside one of the cabins and the only one around, he ordered me to haul him up. At the time, as I felt quite content with the world, I subdued the tendency to tell him where to go, agreed and hauled him to the top of the mast, dutifully holding the rope until he had finished. In the meantime, I was admiring a beautiful yacht coming into the harbour and did not hear his shout the first time that he was finished. He started yelling expletives regarding my parentage and nationality so, instead of descending slowly, he came down at a rate of knots. As he hit the deck, he raced towards me with the silly notion that he could do me harm. As he came abreast, I picked him up and threw him into the harbour.

Pretty sure that my days at the boatyard were numbered, I made my way to the office and asked the manager for my cards. Plainly surprised and sorry that I wanted to leave, he asked for my reasons. I asked him to look out of the window and he would see that the figure trudging up the dyke with water running from the arse of his trousers was the general foreman and I was the immediate cause of his condition. The foreman stormed into the office and keeping a safe distance, demanded that I was finished. To my surprise, the manager refused to sack me and told both of us to keep away from each other.

Eventually, 9th October came around. With Bobby, my eldest brother, as best man, Molly and I were married. We finally moved into the house in May 1947 and it was a marvellous feeling to walk through the door with the lovely smell of new furniture, carpets and paint. The delay had been worthwhile.

Molly in all her bridal glory.

19 Back in uniform as a Territorial

I'VE ALWAYS kept myself busy and my civilian life was quickly full of activities. With Charlie Betts and a few other lads, we formed a life saving club on Sandown beach and, through the auspices of the Royal Life Saving Society, gained all the necessary badges required to set ourselves up as a bona fide body. The following summer, we entered the competition open to all clubs on the South coast, which included life saving races. We had to travel to Weymouth, Southsea and Brighton. We emerged victors. Shortly after that, I joined the Territorials Princess Beatrice Isle of Wight Rifles, which was shortly to be changed from an Anti-Aircraft Artillery Regiment to a Missile Regiment. I refused to have anything to do with guns and decided I wanted to learn about Radar. In two years, I had risen to Sergeant and was instructor in the use of Radar on missile sites. Charlie Betts joined as well, even Bob McAlister had a go – it was a little Commando trio. Charlie and I served for about 14 years, gaining the Long Service Medal, before we decided to call it quits.

During this time, I became Chairman of the Sandown Social Club, which was non- political. The Club was in the doldrums, losing money, and unsavoury characters seemed to rule the roost. At an Annual General Meeting, I was voted in as Chairman and with the help of Charlie Betts and a few others and within a year, the Club was on its feet and a nice place to spend some time.

I first met Charlie during the early days of the forming of Royal Marines Commando. Charlie ended up in A Company, myself in X Company, and by luck, we were usually together on exercises. When we moved to the Isle of Wight, both companies were billeted in Sandown, so we got to know each other very well. As sixty years have passed, it is quite safe to talk about his exploits with the ladies. He always managed to worm his way into the affections of married ones, whose unfortunate husbands were away on military service. It all came to an end, one extremely cold winter's night, when the husband of the lady he was with, came home on leave unexpectedly about midnight. Picture what happened next. Grabbing all his clothes, clad only in his underpants, and for some reason, wearing his socks he was out of the window, and running at a rate of knots up Avenue Road, into Victoria Road, where he was billeted with Mrs Kemp. To his consternation, he found that the front door was locked, as he had lied to his good landlady that he would be out all night on an

A fine show of brawn – and beauty. Sandown Life Guard Corp with our ladies.

Sergeant James Farmer – me – in a new rig. Now in a Royal Artillery Missile Regiment and an instructor on Radar.

exercise. (Too true). In his own words, "I had turned blue with cold, and had no feeling in my feet". He rang the bell, and eventually she came to the door, enquiring, who was at the door at this time of night, and on hearing Charlie on the other side, opened, and after inspecting the sorry sight in front of her, ordered him into the kitchen, and demanded an explanation. He had to endure the same remonstrations almost to the letter, that I had experienced with Pearl Vanner. Mrs Kemp being just as soft as all the other landladies, Charlie ended up with a cup of cocoa, and a dreadful warning as to what happens to young lads who consort with trollops. It taught him a lesson, and soon after he met Kath, who he eventually married after the war.

Charlie was a miscreant in many ways, but he was a first class soldier. One morning Charlie was brought out in front of his platoon, and told that he was now a Lance-Corporal, and would take his platoon for a ten minute drill. On reaching the corner of Royal Crescent, he suddenly gave the order, "Last one at the Chocolate Box, pays". On the disappearance of the platoon, there was an angry shout from the platoon commander. His promotion had lasted approximately 20 seconds. When we moved back to Scotland, as A Troop were billeted quite a few miles away from us I didn't see much of him, but during our sojourn in Sicily and Italy, our paths crossed far too often, and usually ended up in trouble. {I wonder why.} Sadly, at the battle for Brac, Charlie was severely wounded, and not wanting to be taken prisoner, struggled back to the landing craft, although suffering from loss of blood. I did not see him till I came home to Sandown on leave. Charlie was forced to leave the Royal Marines due to his wounds. Our friendship lasted throughout the years. Sadly his wounds got the better of him and he died at the age of 52. A wonderful lad, a wonderful man, a marvellous friend.

20 I take the plunge and set up on my own and 40 Royal Marines Commando Association (1942-1946) comes into being

IT WAS in the late 1950s that I decided to work for myself. With a generous loan of £150 from the bank and a shed in the garden, I took the chance of all self-employed – do well or go under! With plenty of work, especially sign-writing, our standard of living was enough to leave Fitzroy Street and buy a large property in Station Avenue, which Molly used as a guest house for about fifteen years. By this time we had three children, David, Julie and Gary. Then we sold it for the type of home we had always wanted – a large-ish house in Grove Road with a garden and greenhouses, which made Molly very happy. We lived there for nearly twenty years and then Molly died of cancer. I no longer wanted to live there and as my business premises were in Ryde, where Julie and Gary also lived, I sold up and bought a flat there. David sadly died in a car accident when he was only twenty-one. I still find it hard to talk or think about it.

When '40' finally broke up in Basingstoke, some may have thought they would never see the likes of us again. How wrong they were! When Major Houghton, captured at Dieppe was released from prisoner of war camp, he became Commanding Officer of '44' Royal Marines Commando. He persuaded the powers that be that '44' be changed to '40', perpetuating our wonderful war record. It is still very much in existence to this day, carrying on the magnificent service of all Royal Marines Commando units.

In the mid 1950s, the Globe and Laurel journal of the Royal Marines had an article regarding the annual reunion of the Army Commando Association at Portchester Hall in London, stating that Royal Marine Commandos were welcome as associate members. The jungle drums started to beat and at our first get together, over

I TAKE THE PLUNGE AND SET UP ON MY OWN – 40 RMCA COMES IN TO BEING

I pay my respects at the Spean Bridge RM memorial in Scotland.

forty came and it was marvellous to see many old friends again. Many of us kept faith and returned every year though by the end of the 1970's we had found a pub run by a Royal Marine and decided to meet there every year. Through those years, some of us went to Spean Bridge on Remembrance Sunday to the Commando Memorial to pay our respects, staying in Fort William for the weekend.

At our reunion in April 1984 Ken Morris proposed that next year we should organise a reunion that is worthy of us, stop this tradition of males only, invite our wives and spend a weekend together and enjoy ourselves. The place to spend our weekend should be on the Isle of Wight where we had been made welcome as young marines and formed a deep friendship with the Island people, and so 40 Royal Marines Commando Association (1942-46) was launched. Our first reunion soon came round and I can remember that about eighty arrived with wives and luckily there were no hiccups. Ken Morris and Alan Saunders took over the reins of keeping us together and we all decided to return the following year.

143

While I was writing these memoirs Peter Fisher, our splendid secretary gave me plenty of advice, forever jogging my memory, and stating "It is not just about Jock Farmer, it is about all the 40 lads, as what happened to one happened to all". After the '04 Reunion, we decided to make Northern Italy our last pilgrimage to pay respects to our fallen. Peter, with the sterling aid of George Quin, prepared a complicated plan, involving planes, hotels, etc. It was a great success. At our committee meeting in November, I noticed a subtle change in Peter. He looked pre-occupied, and had a slight cough. A week later, he told me rather hoarsely, that he was losing his voice. Shortly after, he was diagnosed with cancer, moved to Bristol, spent just over a week there, and was sent home. Peter died on 17th February 2005. At the beginning of April 2005, it would have been the 20th anniversary of the formation of 40 Royal Marines Commando Association, (1942-1946), and Peter had already laid the groundwork for the programme for 2005.

In the last years of his life, Peter lived in Taunton, a stone's throw away from 40 Commando Royal Marines base at Norton Manor Camp. He became almost a daily visitor, asking, cajoling, wheedling, for all types of help, and support for the veterans, which was always freely given. During the funeral service, Major Spike Kelly spoke warmly of Peter, as being a pain in the backside at times but everything he asked was always for the benefit of the veterans, never for himself. The high esteem that 40 Royal Marines Commando held for Peter was evident at his full military funeral. Six young Royal Marines carried Peter's coffin, and at the appropriate time there was a six gun salute. All Royal Marines, young and old, were at that moment intensely aware of the marvellous bond that existed between us all. Peter arrived in Shanklin, early in January '43, and although we were 'chalk and cheese', as you might say - myself with a broad Scottish accent, and Peter with a rather clipped English voice, we became good friends. During our war, he was a typical '40' lad, highly professional in all that he was asked to do, and imbued with the same trust that was present in all of us.

The late Colonel Neil Maude visited Shanklin Chine in the 1970's to show his wife where he had trained with 40 Royal Marine Commando as a junior officer in 1942. He was sorry to find there was nothing to commemorate their time there. The late Geoffrey Hayles, Manager of the Chine, suggested a memorial. With the active and enthusiastic cooperation of Mrs Anne Springman, owner of the Chine, this idea was adopted. Then began the fruitful partnership between Anne and the Association which continues to flourish. It was in 1984 that the first memorial was built, only to be destroyed in the 1987 hurricane.

I built the present memorial outside the Heritage Centre, well known for the exhibitions staged in the large conservatory and tearoom I built for Anne. Our memorial has now been restyled and refurbished by my son Gary. This is the focus of our Reunion Weekends, with a service of Remembrance attended every spring by our veterans and their wives and families. We cherish this highly personal shrine, where we can pay our respects to our "absent friends". There are also two memorial seats and our flag flies above. Nor is it only here that we remember our old friends.

Peter Fisher had diligently researched and located every one of the graves of our chums fallen in battle and pilgrimages were arranged for those who could manage it to visit them all. In October 2001 Italian Job Mk2 was planned to follow closely 40 Commando's progress from Sicily to Termoli, laying wreaths on every grave. Detailed travel arrangements and plans of each cemetery were produced by Peter and George Quin, with the site of each grave named. The meticulous staff work done by Peter and George was up to the highest standard of 40 Commando performance.

The sixtieth anniversary of the disastrous landings at Dieppe of 19th August 1942 was marked by a series of events attended by a party of twenty veterans and a hundred family and friends of our Association plus a large contingent of the other units who had taken part in this operation. For me it was an emotional pilgrimage which revived memories and recollections of comrades who did not survive. It was our good fortune to be accompanied by Mrs Anne Springman and her husband, Michael. Anne wore her uniform as High Sheriff of the Isle of Wight. I believe this was the first time a High Sheriff had attended an event in uniform in a foreign country. Her presence celebrated the important part Shanklin Chine and the Isle of Wight had played in '40' Commandos' training for Dieppe. In a final and touching private ceremony for '40' Commando Mrs Springman laid a basket of flowers fresh from the Chine on the memorial.

The reception of the whole contingent by the people of Dieppe was overwhelming. The Royal Marine Band added colour and dignity to the various wreath-laying ceremonies. I felt proud to have been among the forces, largely Canadian who suffered so grievously on that day – sixty years ago.

There were countless thousands of young men conscripted into the three services during the war. Every variation of the human race was included; the educated, uneducated, rich, poor, gregarious, shy, religious. The only common bond between them was being declared fit to serve irrespective of their ability to cope with service life. But the most surprising find about '40' was that although all the types just described were contained in the unit, there must have been something extra in our makeup or genes, for the finished article could be described in one word 'dedicated'.

I have only used my chums' names sparingly during my writing, but one lad, Tommy Gray, I must write about. Tommy was a devout Roman Catholic and, as one would expect, a bit on the quiet side. Whenever possible, on a Sunday he would attend the local church, though I don't suppose he understood one word the priest was saying. He neither smoked nor drank, the antithesis of everybody around him, but was one of the most liked. It was quite usual on pay nights, if there were one or two missing at midnight, Tommy would scour the drinking dens, find them and bring them back home.

One evening, I decided to stay in the billet to write some letters and, by chance, Tommy was the only other one present. After a while, I asked him a direct question. "What made you

I TAKE THE PLUNGE AND SET UP ON MY OWN – 40 RMCA COMES IN TO BEING

To mark the 60th Anniversary of the Dieppe Raid in 2002, all the units who made up the attacking force sent contingents of veterans and relatives to a mass commemorative weekend. '40' Commando RM were there in force. General Robert Houghton is shown leading us in a parade through the town. Wreaths were laid on the graves of all our comrades who died on that awful day.

As those who were lost at sea have no known graves, I was privileged to cast a single red rose into the sea as a symbol of our remembrance of them.

147

volunteer for such a unit as this?" He replied, "Hitler and all his colonels belong to the devil and what better way to fight him?"

It was during the fight on the Garigliano, the day after I was wounded, during an advance against German defences, that Tommy was killed. When everybody was back at Vico Equense, somebody asked: "Who the hell is going to look after us on Friday nights now"? It wasn't meant as a joke, rather a plaintive cry from everybody, lamenting the terrible loss of a much liked and respected person.

What a privilege it has been to be a member of '40' Royal Marine Commando.

James 'Jock' Farmer 1921-2006